THE CHILDREN'S
ATLAS OF THE
HUMAN
BODY

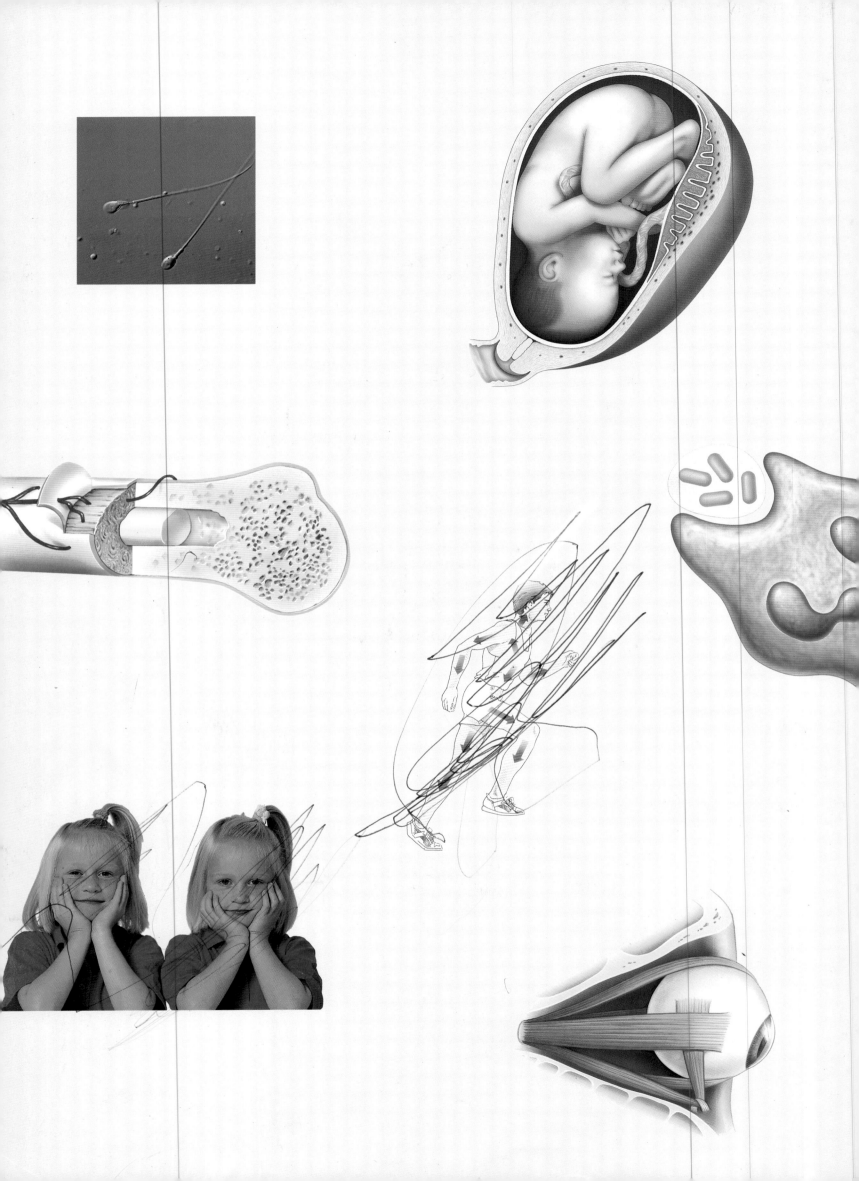

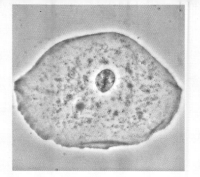

THE CHILDREN'S
ATLAS OF THE
HUMAN
BODY

ACTUAL SIZE BONES, MUSCLES, AND
ORGANS IN FULL COLOR

RICHARD WALKER

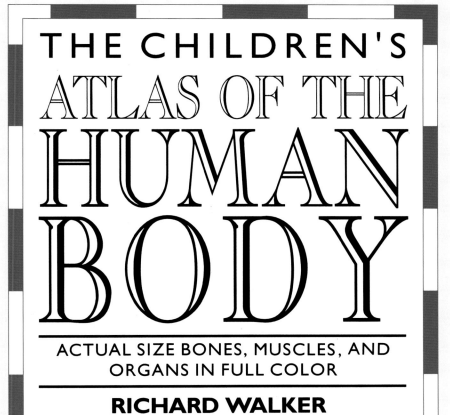

The Millbrook Press
Brookfield, Ct.

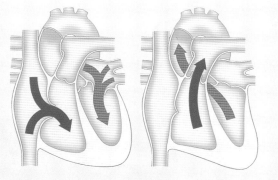

A QUARTO BOOK

First published in the United States of America in 1994 by
The Millbrook Press Inc.
2 Old New Milford Road
Brookfield, Connecticut 06804

Library of Congress Cataloging-in-Publication Data

Walker, Richard.
    The children's atlas of the human body/by Richard Walker.
      p.   cm.
    "A Quarto book"—T.p. verso.
    Includes index.
    ISBN 1-56294-503-3 (lib. bdg.)
    1. Human anatomy—Atlases—Juvenile literature. [1. Human
anatomy. 2. Body, Human.] I. Title.
QM27.W35 1994
611—dc20
                                 93-41527 AC
                                     CIP

This book was produced by:
Quarto Children's Books Ltd
The Fitzpatrick Building
188–194 York Way
London N7 9QP

Managing Editor: Christine Hatt
Editor: Nigel Cawthorne
Designer: Graham Davis
Illustrators: Michael Courtney, Chris Forsey, Rob Shone;
Frank Kennard (poster)
Photographer: Paul Forrester
Picture Research: Sarah Risley

Manufactured by Bright Arts (Pte) Ltd, Singapore.
Printed by Star Standard Industries (Pte) Ltd, Singapore.
Library binding in USA by Horowitz/Rae Book Manufacturers, Inc.

Contents

Life-size human anatomy chart

Humans

Congratulations! You belong to an exclusive club with over five and a half billion members worldwide. That club is the human species, *Homo sapiens*. By looking at any of your fellow members, you can see immediately that they, like you, are human, whichever city, country, island, or continent they may come from. But look closer. They may appear similar, but you can also tell these humans apart. Differences in outward appearance help you recognize family, friends, and the famous. They belong to one of two sexes – male or female. They may also be tall or short, have light or dark skin, be thin or fat. But despite these slight variations you can identify them as humans first and individuals second.

Under the skin

How does a car work? You cannot really tell just by looking at the outside. You need to get under the hood, look at the parts of the engine, and see how they fit together.

The same applies to the human body. Looking from the outside, all you can see is an outer covering of skin. Even looking into the mouth and down the throat does not tell you very much. But under this outer layer lies a collection of different parts that collaborate to produce the complex organism called the human being.

The Children's Atlas of the Human Body gets under the skin, looks at all these vital body parts, and explains clearly what they do and how they work together.

In the small intestine, food is digested and absorbed. In the large intestine waste material is transported out of the body (see pages 32–33).

The femur, or thigh bone, is the longest bone in the body. As part of the skeleton it helps support the body's weight (see pages 14–15).

The femoral artery carries oxygen-rich blood to all parts of the leg (see pages 20–21).

When an egg is fertilized by a sperm, it grows and develops into a baby inside the uterus (see pages 52–55).

The cerebrum is the control center for all body activities (see pages 36–37).

The scapula, or shoulder blade, is the part of the skeleton where the humerus, or upper arm bone, attaches to the body (see pages 14–15).

The kidney filters waste out of the blood and sends it on its way out of the body in the form of urine (see pages 34–35).

Below the back of the cerebrum lies the cerebellum, which ensures that all body movements are smooth and coordinated (see pages 36–37).

The spinal cord connects the brain with the rest of the body (see pages 38–39).

Inside the lung, life-giving oxygen is taken into the bloodstream in exchange for the waste product carbon dioxide (see pages 24–27).

Facial muscles enable humans to subtly change the shape of their face in order to communicate a wide range of emotions (see pages 50–51).

Lying just below the brain, the pituitary gland produces chemical messengers called hormones that control many body activities (see pages 48–49).

Gray matter, which covers the outer part of the cerebrum, is the region where thinking, remembering, and feeling all occur (see pages 36–37).

The nose is the entrance to the respiratory system. Inside it are smell sensors that enable humans to detect odors (see pages 26–27 and 46–47).

Salivary glands release saliva on to food when it enters the mouth to be chewed and swallowed (see pages 28–29).

The aorta, the body's largest artery, carries oxygen-rich blood from the heart to the body (see pages 20–23).

The heart is a muscular pump that sends blood to, and receives blood from, all parts of the body (see pages 22–23).

The ovary normally releases one egg each month, and produces hormones that control the menstrual cycle (see pages 48–49 and 52–53).

The pancreas has two functions: It produces enzymes that help the digestive process in the small intestine; and it releases hormones that control glucose levels in the blood (see pages 32–33 and 48–49).

The body's largest vein, the vena cava, carries oxygen-poor blood to the heart from the rest of the body (see pages 20–23).

The gluteus maximus is a powerful skeletal muscle that enables humans to climb, jump, and run (see pages 16–17).

The sciatic nerve carries nerve impulses from the spinal cord to the leg and foot (see pages 38–39).

Body systems

Think about someone kicking a football. The muscles pull on the leg bones to produce the kicking movement. In order to pull, muscles need energy. This is supplied, in the form of food and oxygen, by the bloodstream. The food is absorbed into the body through the intestines. The oxygen is absorbed through the lungs. Waste material produced by this body activity is removed via the lungs and the urine. And all of this is controlled by messages sent along the nervous system and by chemicals called hormones released into the bloodstream.

Just this one activity illustrates most of the body's systems at work. These major systems support the body, move it, control its activities, transport materials around it, remove waste from it, supply it with oxygen and food, and enable it to reproduce itself. Each has its job to do, but all work together in a coordinated way to produce the intricate complexity of the living human body.

Body systems work together somewhat like the parts of a city. The brain and the nervous system are the city council and telecommunication system. The digestive system provides food, like the stores and supermarkets. The blood system acts like a road network. And the body, like the city, needs its power supplied and its waste disposed.

BODY TOWN

City – body

Administration – brain

Food distribution – digestive system

Roads – bloodstream

Telephone system – nervous system

Waste disposal – urinary system

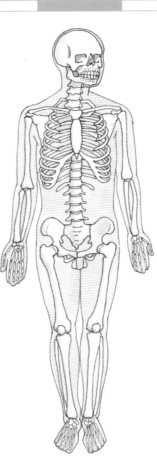

SKELETAL SYSTEM
The skeleton's 206 bones support the body, providing a flexible frame-work that is moved by muscles. Some bones protect delicate organs.

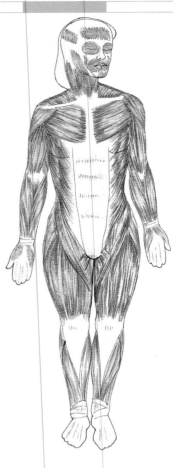

MUSCULAR SYSTEM
Over 600 muscles move the body by pulling bones. Other types of muscle are found in body organs such as the heart and bladder.

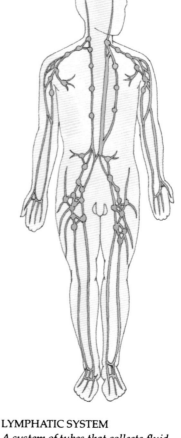

LYMPHATIC SYSTEM
A system of tubes that collects fluid leaking from blood vessels, and drains it back into the blood. Lymph nodes filter out any harmful germs.

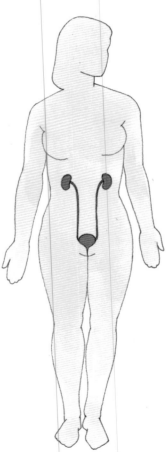

URINARY SYSTEM
Two kidneys filter the blood, removing waste and excess water. The product, urine, is stored in the bladder before release from the body.

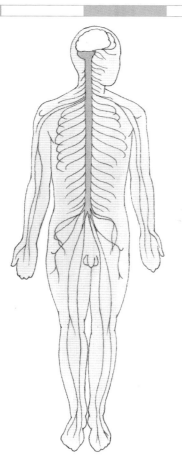
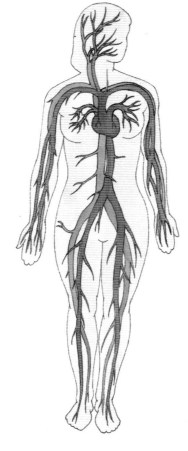

NERVOUS SYSTEM
This rapid response system co-ordinates body activities. Its control center, the brain, receives and sends out messages along the nerves.

CIRCULATORY SYSTEM
The heart pumps blood around a network of blood vessels. This supplies all body parts with oxygen and food, and removes waste.

RESPIRATORY SYSTEM
The respiratory system extracts oxygen from air breathed into the lungs, exchanging it for carbon dioxide, which is breathed out.

DIGESTIVE SYSTEM
Food is needed for growth and repair, as well as for energy. The digestive system breaks down food and absorbs it, so it can be used.

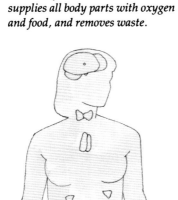
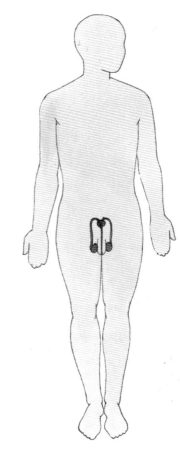
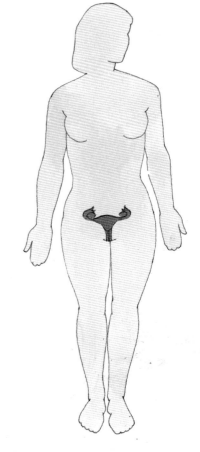

HORMONAL SYSTEM
Hormones, produced by endocrine glands, control many body processes. The nervous and hormonal systems work closely together.

REPRODUCTIVE SYSTEM
The job of the reproductive system is to produce children. The male testes produce sperm that fertilize eggs produced in the female's ovaries.

Building blocks

The body's building blocks are called cells. However, unlike bricks, the building blocks of a house, cells are too small to see individually. Even the tiniest dot you can make with a pen is much bigger than the biggest of your body's cells, and your body is made up of over a trillion of them.

Each one of these cells is a single living unit. It contains all the instructions it needs to construct another cell just like it. It has the means to manufacture most of the materials it needs and ways of importing those it cannot. It has the capacity to eject waste products and the ability to generate the energy it needs to power all its activities. And cells do not work alone. They have ways of acting in concert with their neighbors. So when you put them all together, you get a walking, talking human being – just like you.

INSIDE THE CELL
Cells may be small, but they are not simple. Each is packed with tiny components called organelles. Controlled by the nucleus, the organelles work together to keep the cell alive and working properly.

Centrioles – involved in cell division

Mitochondrion – releases energy to power cell activities

Nucleus – controls cell activities

Lysosome – contains digestive chemicals used to break down and recycle worn-out parts of the cell

Ribosome – makes important chemicals called proteins

Golgi body – processes proteins, preparing some for export

THE CELL AS A COUNTRY
The components of a cell are like the parts of a country. The nucleus is the government. The mitochondria are the power stations. The endoplasmic reticulum is the road network. The ribosomes are the factories. And the outer membrane is the country's border with its immigration checkpoints or customhouses.

Cell membrane – outer boundary which allows certain substances to pass in or out of the cell

Cytoplasm – liquid part of cell in which all other parts are suspended

THE MASTER MOLECULE
Inside the nucleus are long molecules that resemble twisted ladders. These are DNA molecules and contain, in code, all the information needed to construct and run a living cell.

TYPES OF CELLS

Most of the body's billions of cells do not look like the "typical" cell (below left), although they contain the same components. What a cell looks like depends on what it does.

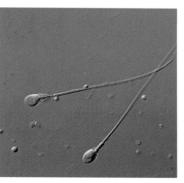

Sperm are streamlined cell "missiles" that swim, propelled by beating "tails," to fertilize an egg.

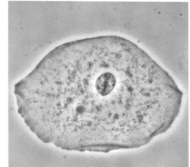

Cheek cells are flat. They form a moist, flexible, protective layer inside the mouth.

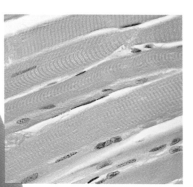

Skeletal muscle cells move the body. They are long, thin, and work by contracting (getting shorter).

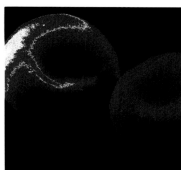

Red blood cells are disc-shaped. They carry oxygen around the body, through the smallest blood vessels.

Endoplasmic reticulum – transports materials throughout the cell

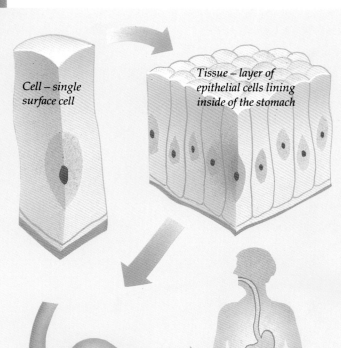

Cell – single surface cell

Tissue – layer of epithelial cells lining inside of the stomach

Organ – all the tissues making up the stomach

System – all the organs making up the digestive system

FROM CELL TO PERSON

The body is made up of cells, but all cells are not the same. Groups of cells of one particular type are packed together to form a tissue. Different types of tissue work together to form an organ, such as the stomach. A number of organs link up to form a system, such as the digestive system. All of these systems together make up the body.

13

Skeleton

The word "skeleton" comes from the ancient Greek for "dried up" – not a very good description for the living, engineering marvel that supports and shapes you. Your skeleton is made up of 206 bones that are linked together to form a strong, but light, supporting framework. And bones are alive. The hard outside is made of tough fibers and minerals such as calcium, and living cells with their own supply of blood and nerves.

But, the skeleton is much more than a support system. Bones provide an anchorage for muscles, allowing us to stand, walk, jump, and run. Some bones, like the skull and ribs, protect delicate organs such as the brain and heart. The network of bones in your hands, which contains a quarter of the bones in your body, enables you to perform delicate movements like writing or sewing. The inner core of bones, the soft marrow, produces millions of blood cells each day.

INSIDE A BONE
Look inside a bone and you will see that it is not solid. The shaft is hollow, filled with bone marrow, and the end of the bone is honeycombed with spaces. This makes the bone both strong and light. Bone is six times stronger than a steel bar of the same weight.

FROM SKULL TO TOE BONE
The skull, backbone, and ribcage form the central core of the skeleton. Fixed to the backbone are the shoulder and hip bones. The arm bones are attached to the shoulder bones, and the leg bones are attached to the hip bones. All bones are held together by tough straps of fibrous tissue called ligaments.

Compact bone　　*Marrow*　　*Spongy bone*

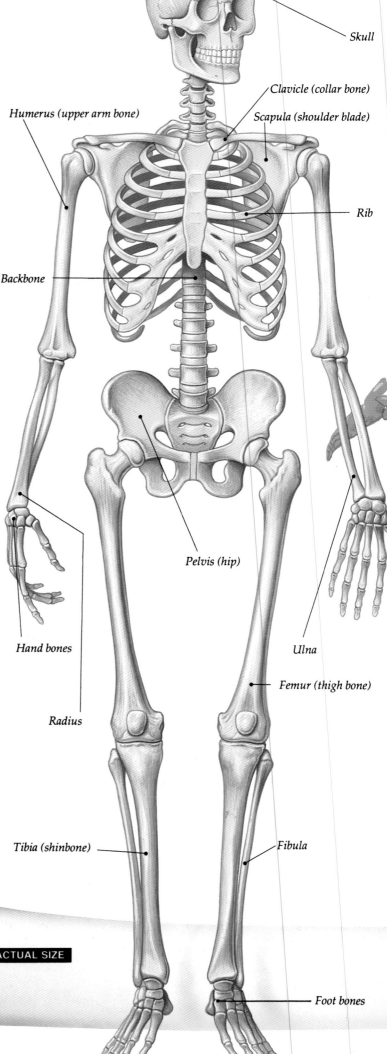

Skull

Clavicle (collar bone)

Humerus (upper arm bone)

Scapula (shoulder blade)

Rib

Backbone

Pelvis (hip)

Hand bones

Ulna

Femur (thigh bone)

Radius

Tibia (shinbone)

Fibula

● ACTUAL SIZE

Foot bones

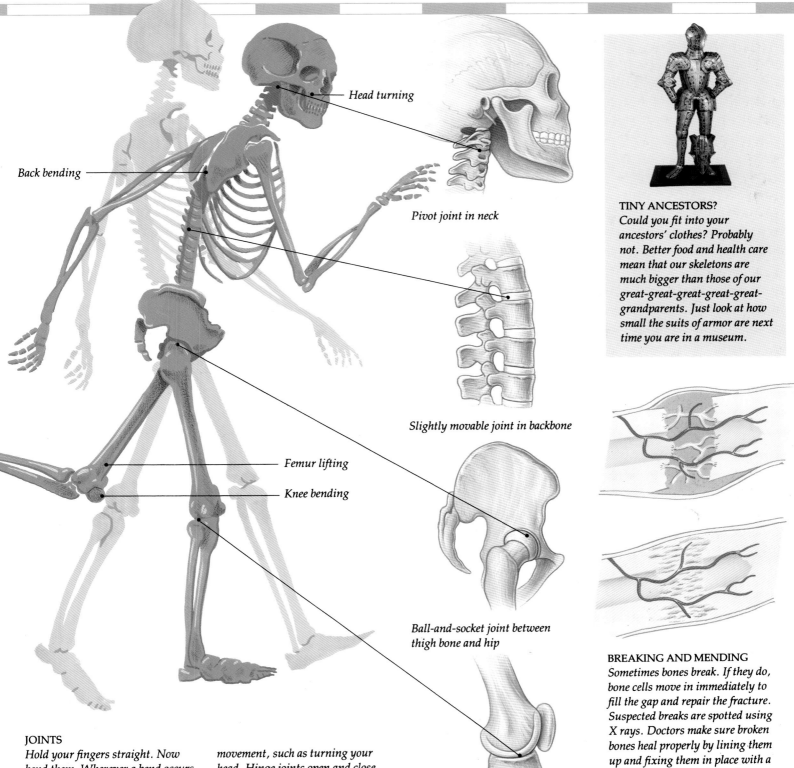

Head turning

Pivot joint in neck

Back bending

Slightly movable joint in backbone

Femur lifting

Knee bending

Ball-and-socket joint between
thigh bone and hip

Hinge joint in knee

Stirrup

TINY ANCESTORS?
Could you fit into your ancestors' clothes? Probably not. Better food and health care mean that our skeletons are much bigger than those of our great-great-great-great-great-grandparents. Just look at how small the suits of armor are next time you are in a museum.

BREAKING AND MENDING
Sometimes bones break. If they do, bone cells move in immediately to fill the gap and repair the fracture. Suspected breaks are spotted using X rays. Doctors make sure broken bones heal properly by lining them up and fixing them in place with a plaster cast, or by bolting them together. Broken bones take about three months to heal.

JOINTS
Hold your fingers straight. Now bend them. Wherever a bend occurs there is a joint between the finger bones. In fact, there are joints where all bones meet. Joints enable us to perform all sorts of movements. Pivot joints allow a turning movement, such as turning your head. Hinge joints open and close like a door hinge. Ball-and-socket joints allow all-around movement like that of a computer joystick. Other joints, such as those in the backbone, move only slightly.

SHORTEST AND LONGEST
The shortest bones are the three ossicles found in your ear. The smallest of these is the stirrup bone, at a little more than an eighth of an inch (3 mm) long. The longest bone is the femur in your thigh. It provides the main support for your weight.

Muscles

Muscles make movement possible. A dancer's pirouette, the change in the size of your pupils, an artist's brush strokes, your heartbeat, swallowing food, breathing, or running a marathon – all are caused by muscles. Muscles work by pulling and are made up of cells that can contract (get shorter). Contraction requires energy, and energy release requires a constant supply of food and oxygen. This explains why, when muscles are working hard during exercise, your heart rate speeds up, increasing blood flow so that more food and oxygen are supplied to the muscles.

The muscles you are most aware of are skeletal muscles, the ones that move your body. Skeletal muscles are firmly linked to bones by tough, inelastic tendons. These muscles are under voluntary control – that is, they do what they are told. When they receive a message from the brain, they contract and pull on the bones they are attached to. Other types of muscles work automatically, whether you are asleep or awake. These are the involuntary muscles and are found in the intestines, bladder, and other parts of the body. The brain tells them what to do without your being aware of it. Another type of involuntary muscle in the heart makes it beat by itself.

TEAMWORK
The muscles that move your skeleton work in pairs. The reason for this is simple. Muscles pull, but they cannot push. To bend the arm, for example, the biceps muscle pulls the forearm up. To straighten the arm, the biceps' teammate, the triceps, pulls the forearm down. Feel this for yourself. Your upper arm muscles get fatter as they pull, or contract, and thinner as they relax.

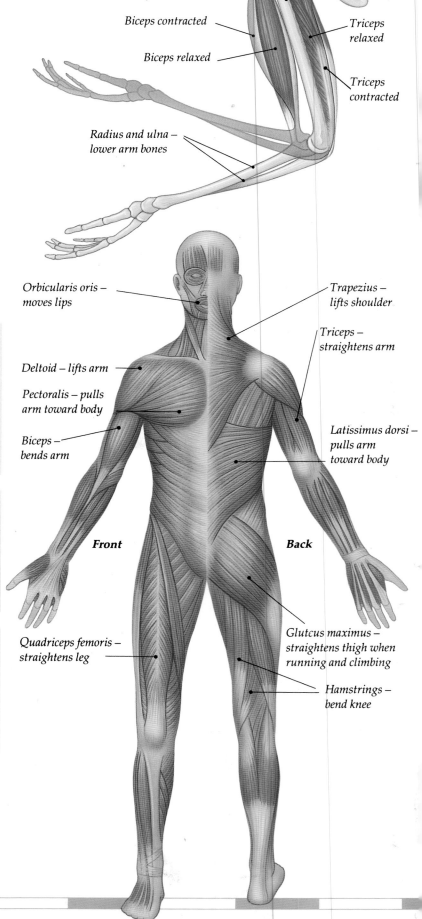

Humerus – upper arm bone

Tendon

Biceps contracted

Biceps relaxed

Triceps relaxed

Triceps contracted

Radius and ulna – lower arm bones

Orbicularis oris – moves lips

Trapezius – lifts shoulder

Triceps – straightens arm

Deltoid – lifts arm

Pectoralis – pulls arm toward body

Biceps – bends arm

Latissimus dorsi – pulls arm toward body

Front

Back

Quadriceps femoris – straightens leg

Glutcus maximus – straightens thigh when running and climbing

Hamstrings – bend knee

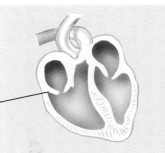

Cardiac muscle in the heart

Smooth muscle in the esophagus

Skeletal muscle

TYPES OF MUSCLE
The body contains three types of muscle. Skeletal muscle moves the skeleton. Smooth muscle contracts rhythmically, and automatically, moving food along the digestive system, squeezing urine out of the bladder, *or pushing a baby out of the womb during birth. And cardiac muscle, found only in the heart, contracts non-stop throughout your life and pumps blood around your body.*

MUSCLES IN ACTION
Put your finger in your mouth and bite it – but not too hard! The pain you feel is caused by the massive squeezing power of the masseter and temporalis muscles (right). Both are attached to the skull, at one end, and the lower jaw at the other. When they contract, the jaws and teeth clamp shut around food, enabling you to tear off chunks. To feel them contract, press your fingers just below the cheek bones and clench your teeth.

MAJOR MUSCLES
There are around 640 skeletal muscles in the body. The largest is the gluteus maximus in the buttocks and thighs. The tiniest is the stapedius in the ear, which is just over .04 inch (1 mm) long. Some major muscles are shown here (left). Each muscle moves a specific part of the body. Which muscle contracts when, and with what force, is coordinated by the brain. This is why we are able to walk, sit, stand, dance, run, write, paint, sculpt, or juggle.

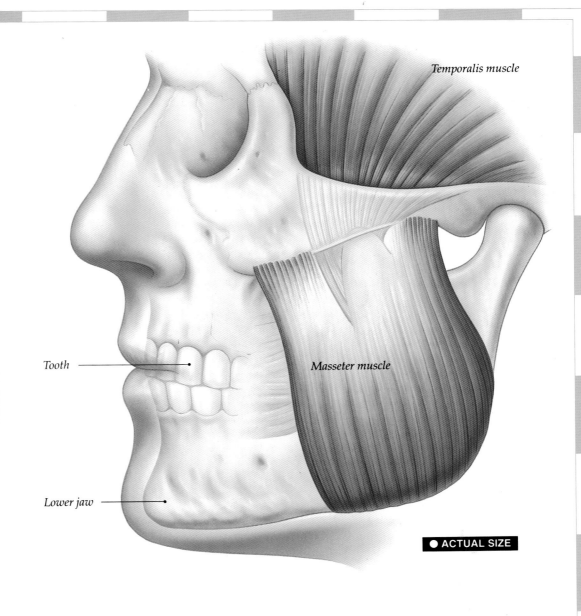

Temporalis muscle

Tooth

Masseter muscle

Lower jaw

● ACTUAL SIZE

INSIDE A SKELETAL MUSCLE
Like any other tissue in the body, muscles are made up of cells. But muscle cells, or fibers, are rather special. First, they are very long and thin, up to 12 inches (30 cm) long. Second, they can shorten by up to a third of their length when stimulated by a nerve. The parts of the fiber that get shorter are the myofibrils. A bundle of myofibrils runs along the length of each fiber. Myofibrils also give the fiber a stripy appearance – skeletal muscle is sometimes called striped muscle. The fibers themselves run along the length of the muscle and are, in turn, bundled together in fascicles. Bundles of fascicles make up the whole muscle. In all, over 2,000 fibers can make up a single muscle.

Connective tissue surrounding muscle

Fascicle (bundle of muscle fibers)

Muscle

Connective tissue surrounding fascicle

Myofibril

Stripe

Muscle fiber

Blood

Blood looks like simple red liquid, but it is much more than that. It is a complex mixture of cells floating in a watery solution, which contains many other substances. Most of these cells are the red blood cells that give blood its color. There are over 25 trillion of these in the blood. They are produced at the rate of 3 million per second by bone marrow. Each red blood cell survives for about four months. Red blood cells carry out one of the blood's major functions – carrying oxygen from the lungs to the rest of the body. But blood has many other jobs to do. It transports carbon dioxide and other wastes ready to be disposed of away from cells. It supplies cells with food absorbed from the intestines. It carries chemical messengers called hormones. And its white blood cells fight off infection.

CELLS AND PLASMA

Blood is the body's only liquid tissue. Over half of it (55%) consists of a pale yellow liquid called plasma that lets blood flow. The rest (45%) is made up of red and white blood cells.

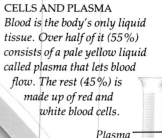

Plasma

Blood cells

IN THE BLOODSTREAM

Imagine you have shrunk until you are tiny enough to swim along a blood capillary. What would you see on your journey? Carried along by the flow you would bounce off the doughnut-shaped red blood cells that take up most of the space. On closer inspection, they look more orange than red. But look out for

smaller objects shaped like potato chips. They are the platelets and are vitally important in stopping bleeding if you are cut. Don't stay too long in the bloodstream, though. One of the white blood cells may eat you. After all, inside the body, you would be considered a highly dangerous invader!

Neutrophil (white blood cell)

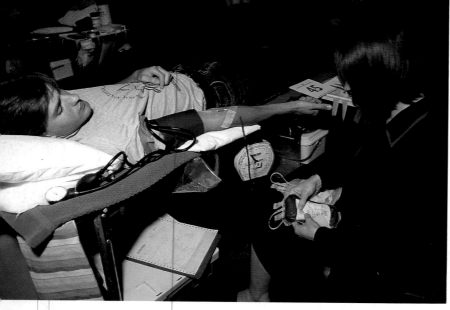

GIVING BLOOD

Sometimes, people lose so much blood through injury that their lives are at risk. But they can be saved by a blood transfusion. Other people's blood is transferred into their bloodstream.

The blood needed for transfusions is given, or donated, at special locations (above). However, before a donor gives blood, the blood group must be checked. Each person belongs to one of four blood groups.

These are the groups A, B, AB, and O. If blood from one group is given to a person of another group it can make them very ill. If they are dangerously ill already, giving them a transfusion of the wrong type of blood could kill them.

Giving blood takes about half an hour. During that time about 1 pint (500 ml) of blood is taken. This is then stored in a blood bank until it is needed.

TYPES OF BLOOD CELLS

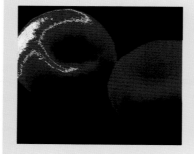

Red blood cells are dimpled discs with no nucleus. They are packed with orange hemoglobin, which picks up oxygen in the lungs and unloads it in the tissues – losing some of its bright color.

Neutrophils are the most numerous white blood cells, with one for every thousand red blood cells. Neutrophils are hunters, seeking out and eating any invading germs.

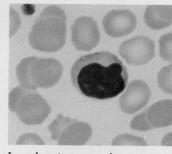

Lymphocytes engage in chemical warfare, producing antibodies that wipe out bacteria and viruses. There is one of these white blood cells for every 2,000 red ones.

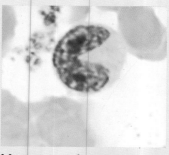

Monocytes are the scourge of any germs invading the body's tissues. These white cells – there is one of these for every 10,000 red cells – hunt and eat all "foreign" particles.

FIGHTING INFECTION

Every second of every day, the body is under attack from the bacteria and viruses that enter the body through the nose and throat, or through cuts in the skin, or in food. Fortunately, the body has two lines of defense to thwart any invaders. First, white blood cells, like the macrophage (below) wander through the body's tissues searching relentlessly for any germs. Once discovered, harmful microorganisms are surrounded, eaten, and digested. Second, other white blood cells, called lymphocytes, produce killer chemicals, called antibodies, that identify and wipe out bacteria and viruses wherever they may be.

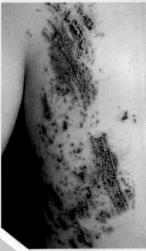

PREVENTING LEAKS

What happens if a pipe bursts at home? All the water leaks out. The same thing happens if you cut yourself and a blood vessel breaks. Fortunately, the body has an automatic system to plug leaks as soon as they happen. This prevents you from bleeding to death.

Plugging leaks works like this. At the site of the wound, a mesh of fibers forms a plug by trapping red blood cells like fish in a fishing net. This plug dries out to form a scab (left) that keeps germs out while the skin is repairing itself underneath.

Bacteria

White blood cell about to engulf, and eat, bacteria

Platelet

Lymphocyte (white blood cell)

Red blood cell

Wall of blood capillary

Plasma

HOW MUCH BLOOD?

How many soft drink cans would your blood fill? If you are an adult female, between 12 and 15, depending on your size. If you are an adult male, you could fill between 15 and 18 cans.

Monocyte (white blood cell)

Blood vessels

Blood vessels are the highways of the body. The major roads are the big arteries and veins that carry blood between heart and body organs. The minor roads are the small arteries and veins that spread out through the tissues. The back alleys and driveways are the capillaries, along which the blood makes its deliveries to, and collections from, the individual cells. To see how the parts of this system fit together, let us follow the journey of a single red blood cell.

This blood cell has just been pumped, with millions of its companions, from the left side of the heart. It travels down the main artery, the aorta, into one of the many smaller arterial branches. These supply the organs, such as the liver and kidneys. Inside the organ the artery branches again and again until, eventually, the blood cell finds itself inside a capillary, which is just wider than the blood cell itself. Now our blood cell begins its return journey, squeezing along capillaries that join to form smaller veins that, in turn, join to form larger veins. Finally, our blood cell enters the right side of the heart through the vena cava, the biggest vein of all. After a detour to the lungs to pick up oxygen, the blood cell sets off for another trip around the circuit.

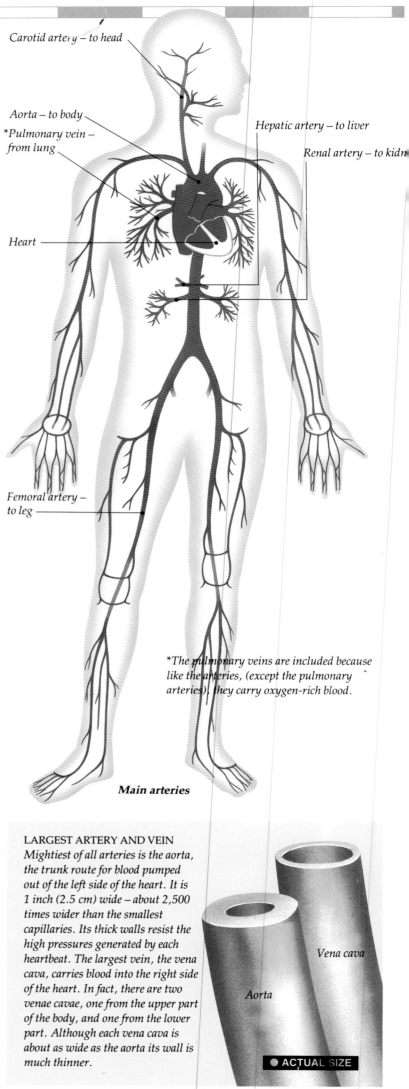

Carotid artery – to head

Aorta – to body

*Pulmonary vein – from lung

Hepatic artery – to liver

Renal artery – to kidney

Heart

Femoral artery – to leg

*The pulmonary veins are included because like the arteries, (except the pulmonary arteries), they carry oxygen-rich blood.

Main arteries

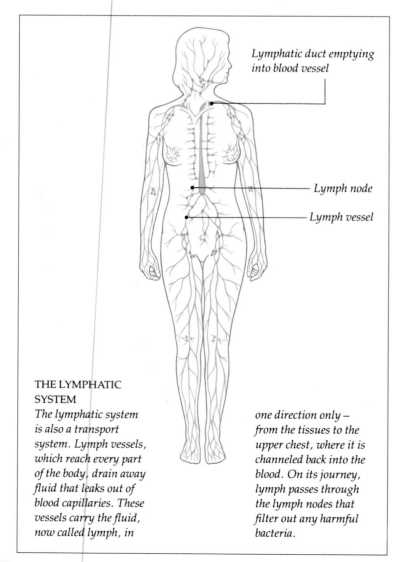

Lymphatic duct emptying into blood vessel

Lymph node

Lymph vessel

THE LYMPHATIC SYSTEM

The lymphatic system is also a transport system. Lymph vessels, which reach every part of the body, drain away fluid that leaks out of blood capillaries. These vessels carry the fluid, now called lymph, in one direction only – from the tissues to the upper chest, where it is channeled back into the blood. On its journey, lymph passes through the lymph nodes that filter out any harmful bacteria.

LARGEST ARTERY AND VEIN

Mightiest of all arteries is the aorta, the trunk route for blood pumped out of the left side of the heart. It is 1 inch (2.5 cm) wide – about 2,500 times wider than the smallest capillaries. Its thick walls resist the high pressures generated by each heartbeat. The largest vein, the vena cava, carries blood into the right side of the heart. In fact, there are two venae cavae, one from the upper part of the body, and one from the lower part. Although each vena cava is about as wide as the aorta its wall is much thinner.

Vena cava

Aorta

● ACTUAL SIZE

*Pulmonary artery – to lung

Jugular vein – from head

Superior vena cava – from upper body

Heart

Inferior vena cava – from lower body

Hepatic vein – from liver

Renal vein – from kidney

Femoral vein – from leg

*The pulmonary arteries are included because like the veins, (except the pulmonary veins), they carry oxygen-poor blood.

Main veins

HOW LONG IS THE SYSTEM?

Imagine all your arteries, veins, and capillaries laid end to end. They would stretch over 60,000 miles (96,000 km). This is one-quarter of the distance from the Earth to the Moon.

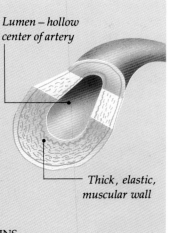

ARTERIES

Arteries carry blood away from the heart. Apart from the pulmonary artery, which takes oxygen-poor blood to the lungs, they all transport oxygen-rich blood. Arteries have tough, thick walls that are both muscular and elastic. These strong walls ensure that arteries do not burst under the high pressure produced by the heart. The largest arteries are as wide as your thumb. The smallest, the arterioles, are no thicker than a piece of thread.

Lumen – hollow center of artery

Thick, elastic, muscular wall

VEINS

Veins carry blood toward the heart. Apart from the pulmonary vein, which carries oxygen-rich blood from the lungs, all veins transport oxygen-poor blood. Veins have valves, to stop blood flowing backward. Their walls are thin because veins are less likely to burst than arteries. The blood inside them is at a lower pressure. Veins range in diameter from around 1 inch (2.5 cm) to that of a fine thread. The tiniest veins are called venules.

Wall of vein, thinner and less muscular than artery

Valve

Lumen – hollow center of vein

LIFE PULSE

Every time the heart contracts, it pushes blood along the arteries. Being elastic, arteries deal with these surges of blood by expanding, then shrinking. This movement is called a pulse. It tells how fast the heart is beating. You can feel your pulse wherever an artery is near the skin's surface. Find the pulse in your wrist (right). Now walk around. The pulse rate will go up as your heart beats faster.

At rest your pulse rate should be 60–80 beats per minute.

CAPILLARIES

Capillaries link arteries and veins. They are tiny, with diameters just big enough to allow red blood cells to pass along them in single file. The wall of a capillary is just one cell thick. Capillary networks form the point of contact between the blood system and body cells. As blood travels through the tissues, along the capillaries, materials such as food and oxygen are supplied to cells, while wastes and other products are removed.

Wall of capillary, one cell thick

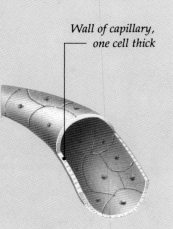

Heart

Why do we talk about broken hearts, or tugging at the heart strings, and draw arrows through hearts when people fall in love? Well, at one time, it was believed that the heart was the center for feelings of love and emotion. We now know that emotions are controlled by the brain, and that the heart is simply a pump that pushes blood around every part of the body. But it is a resilient pump. The cardiac muscle that makes up the heart contracts around 75 times a minute, day and night, sometimes for over 100 years. It beats automatically, without instructions from the brain, only speeding up, or slowing down, with the body's demands. The heart maintains a constant flow of blood to every cell in the body. Without the unceasing supply of food and oxygen that the blood brings, the cells would die.

WHERE IS THE HEART?
The heart lies just left of center in the chest cavity, or thorax, between the lungs. A bony cage, formed by the ribs and breastbone, surrounds and protects both heart and lungs.

OUTSIDE THE HEART
From the outside, the heart looks only slightly like the pink "heart shape" seen on Valentine's cards. Clearly visible on its surface are the coronary arteries and veins, which supply the food and oxygen needed by the heart muscle to maintain its non-stop pumping.

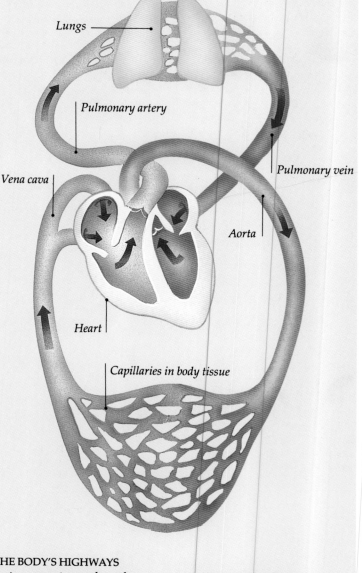

Lungs

Pulmonary artery

Vena cava

Pulmonary vein

Aorta

Heart

Capillaries in body tissue

Vena cava – from body

Aorta – to body

Pulmonary artery – to lungs

Pulmonary vein – from lungs

Left atrium

Right atrium

Left ventricle

Right ventricle

THE BODY'S HIGHWAYS
Just as a country needs road and rail systems to supply its needs, so the body requires its own transport system to service its billions of cells. In the body, this is the circulatory system, a massive network of blood vessels that carries blood everywhere. At its core is the heart. This tireless pump sends blood to the lungs, where it picks up oxygen. Then it sends the blood around the rest of the body, supplying and nurturing the body's cells on its way.

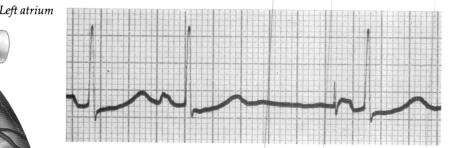

● ACTUAL SIZE

HEART TRACES
As the heart beats, an electric current passes over the heart's surface. This can be picked up by electrodes on the skin, producing a graph, or trace, called an ECG (electrocardiogram). By looking at an ECG, a doctor can tell whether the heart is working properly.

INSIDE THE HEART

The heart has two sides, the left and the right. Each side is divided into two chambers, the upper and the lower. The upper chambers, or atria, have thin walls. They pump blood into the lower chambers, or ventricles, which have thick, muscular walls. The wall of the left ventricle is thicker than the right, however. This is because the left ventricle pumps blood around the body, while the right ventricle only pumps blood the short distance to the lungs. Between each atrium and ventricle is a valve that stops blood flowing backward as the heart beats. There are also valves in the pulmonary artery, where blood leaves the right ventricle, and the aorta, where it leaves the left ventricle.

OPEN HEART SURGERY

Open heart surgery involves cutting into the heart or the vessels that supply it with blood. It is made possible by the use of a heart-lung machine. This takes over the job of pumping blood around the body, and adding oxygen to it, until the operation on the heart has finished.

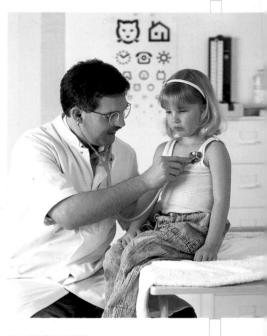

Aorta

Pulmonary artery

Pulmonary vein

Left atrium

Valve

Right atrium

Valve

Left ventricle

Right ventricle

Vena cava

● ACTUAL SIZE

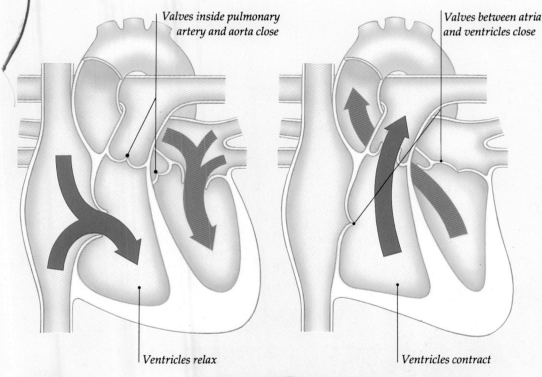

Valves inside pulmonary artery and aorta close

Valves between atria and ventricles close

Ventricles relax

Ventricles contract

PUMPING BLOOD

To imagine how tough and tireless your heart is, clench your fist every second. How long can you keep it up? The muscle in your heart contracts around 100,000 times a day without getting tired. The pumping process takes place in two stages. First, both ventricles

relax. Oxygen-poor blood is drawn into the right ventricle from the body, and oxygen-rich blood into the left ventricle from the lungs. Then both ventricles contract. The valves between atria and ventricles snap shut. Blood is forced from the right ventricle to the lungs, and from the left ventricle to the body.

HEART SOUNDS

Doctors can tell a lot about the heart by listening to the sounds it makes with a stethoscope. A healthy heart makes two sounds: "lub" – which is long and loud – and "dupp" – which is shorter and softer. Through a stethoscope you would hear: "lub-dupp," "lub-dupp" … repeated endlessly. These sounds are produced by the heart valves snapping shut. Unusual heart sounds can tell a doctor that the heart is not pumping properly because its valves are leaking.

Lungs

Every time you breathe, you move air in and out of your lungs. The air you inhale contains around 20 percent oxygen. Some of this oxygen is absorbed into your bloodstream. The blood carries the oxygen to all body cells. Once inside a cell, oxygen is used to burn food and release the energy locked inside it in a process called respiration. This energy is essential to keep the cell alive and functioning normally. Respiration also releases an unwanted waste product called carbon dioxide, which needs to be disposed of. The blood carries this speedily to the lungs where it is breathed out.

Your two lungs are perfectly adapted to their job. They have a rich blood supply, which makes them pink. They also have millions of tiny channels to carry air, which makes them spongy – so spongy, in fact, that together they weigh just 2.2 pounds (1 kilogram) although they have a total volume of 12.7 pints (6 liters).

WHERE ARE THE LUNGS?
The lungs are found in the chest (thorax), and surround the heart. They are connected to the nasal passage by the windpipe (trachea).

OXYGEN SUPPLY
The body's billions of cells demand a non-stop oxygen supply to keep them alive. To satisfy this demand, the heart pumps oxygen-rich blood out to the tissues seventy times a minute – more if you are exercising – in a two-stage process. First, the blood picks up its oxygen supply in the lungs. Then it travels around the body, unloading oxygen as it goes.

Right lung

Blood carries oxygen to all parts of this athlete's body.

SLIPPERY SURFACES
Lungs are not solid lumps of tissue. They are light and spongy, and filled with millions of air channels that are lined with a thin layer of liquid. The presence of so many air spaces provides an enormous surface for absorbing oxygen from the air you breathe in. In fact, if the lungs could be flattened out they would produce a slippery surface the size of a tennis court.

Windpipe (trachea)

High up in the mountains the air is thinner than at sea level. People who live in places with a high altitude have larger lungs so they can take in more air with each breath and get the right amount of oxygen.

● ACTUAL SIZE

Bronchus

Bronchiole

DAMAGED LUNGS
Cigarette smoke turns healthy pink lung tissue black. Chemicals in cigarette smoke can make lung cells cancerous. These cells multiply out of control, causing lung cancer, which usually kills the smoker.

EXCHANGING GASES
Inside your lungs are 600 million alveoli, which are tiny air bags at the ends of the bronchioles. When you breathe in, oxygen moves from the alveoli into the bloodstream. Carbon dioxide which is not needed by the body, moves from the blood into the alveoli and is breathed out.

Oxygen moves into blood

Carbon dioxide moves out of blood

Alveolus

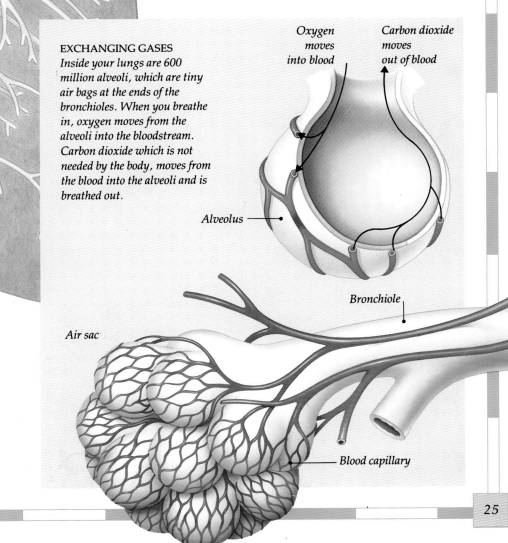

Bronchiole

Air sac

Blood capillary

Left lung (cut open)

INSIDE THE LUNGS
A look inside the lungs reveals a structure resembling an upside down tree. The "trunk" of this tree is the windpipe, or trachea. Its main "branches" are the two bronchi. Each bronchus divides into smaller and smaller branches. The smallest "twigs" of the tree, the bronchioles, are less than .03 inches (1 mm) wide. At the end of bronchioles are clusters of tiny air bags called alveoli.

Breathing

You might be able to live without food for weeks, or without water for days, but breathing is something you have to do, without stopping, every day of your life. Breathing moves air in and out of the lungs, bringing oxygen into the body and removing waste carbon dioxide. You can tell this exchange of gases is happening because the air you breathe in contains about 21 percent oxygen and a tiny amount of carbon dioxide, and the air you breathe out contains less oxygen, about 16 percent, and more carbon dioxide, up to 4 percent.

Breathing can be confusing. You might think your chest is moving because you are breathing. In fact, you are breathing because your chest is moving. The lungs are floppy and passive. They cannot expand on their own. They need the chest to get bigger to expand them and draw air in, and to get smaller to compress them and push the air out again.

THE BREATHING SYSTEM
Air is taken into the breathing system through the nose where it is warmed up and moistened. It travels down the throat, down the windpipe, which is held open by cartilage rings, and into the lungs. The rib cage surrounding the lungs, and the diaphragm below the lungs, cause the chest movements that draw air in and out of the lungs during breathing.

AIR FILTERS
The air you breathe is rarely completely clean, especially in towns and cities. It contains particles of all shapes and sizes, such as dust, grit, and pollen grains. If you breathed these in, they could damage the delicate tissues of the lungs. So the air is automatically filtered as you breathe it. Hairs, and sticky mucus, trap particles inside the nose. Mucus also traps particles along the length of the windpipe. As it does so, the mucus is propelled upward by tiny, hairlike cilia (above) that beat back and forth. When it reaches the throat, it is swallowed.

VENTILATING THE LUNGS
To breathe in, your diaphragm, the muscle at the bottom of the chest, flattens and pushes downward. At the same time, muscles pull your ribs upward and outward. The movements of your diaphragm and ribs expand your chest, sucking air into the lungs from outside. When you breathe out the opposite happens. The diaphragm relaxes and is pushed upward. The ribs move downward and inward. This makes the chest smaller, squeezing air out of the lungs.

BREATHING IN
Ribcage moves upward and outward.

BREATHING OUT
Ribs move downward and inward.

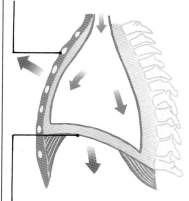

Diaphragm pushes downward. As the chest expands, so do the lungs. Air is sucked into the lungs.

Diaphragm is pushed upward. As the chest gets smaller, so do the lungs. Air is squeezed out of the lungs.

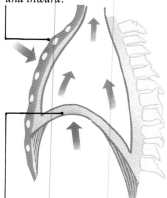

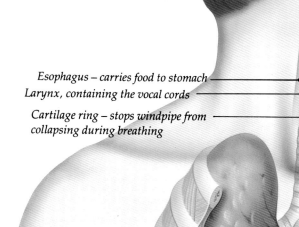

Nasal cavity – air is warmed, cleaned, and moistened here

Throat

Epiglottis – closes entrance to larynx during swallowing

Esophagus – carries food to stomach

Larynx, containing the vocal cords

Cartilage ring – stops windpipe from collapsing during breathing

Windpipe (trachea)

Intercostal muscle – moves ribs

Rib

Right lung

Heart

Diaphragm

Your breathing rate depends on how active you are. At rest you would probably breathe around 15 times each minute. With each breath you would take in about 1 pint (500ml) of air. When you exercise, your breathing rate, and the amount of air taken in, both go up. A sprinting athlete would breathe about 25 times per second. With each breath, he or she would take in five times as much air as normal to keep up with the body's demand for oxygen. A spirometer (right) measures the volume of air breathed in and out.

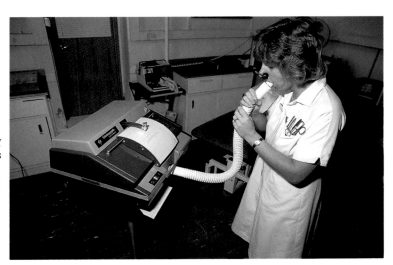

MAKING SOUNDS

You make sounds inside your voice box, or larynx. Stretched across the larynx are the vocal cords (below). When these are nearly closed, and air is forced through them, they vibrate, producing sounds. When tight, they produce high-pitched sounds. When loose, they produce low-pitched sounds.

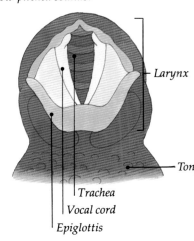

Larynx

Tongue

Trachea

Vocal cord

Epiglottis

UNUSUAL MOVEMENTS

Sneezing, hiccuping, laughing, and coughing (below) are all unusual breathing movements. Sneezing is a sudden release of built-up air pressure which blows dust from your nose. Coughing is a sudden blast of air that clears any particles from the windpipe. Laughing is caused by sudden contractions of the diaphragm, forcing air out in spurts. Hiccups happen when the diaphragm is irritated. It suddenly flattens and sucks in air.

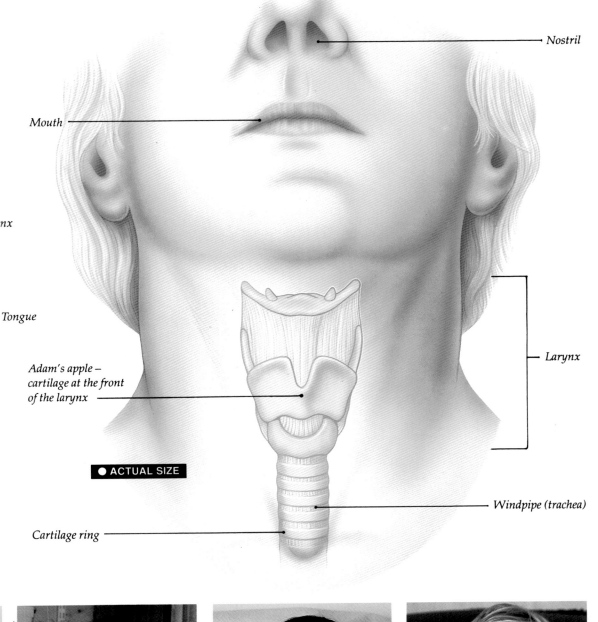

Nostril

Mouth

Adam's apple –
cartilage at the front
of the larynx

Larynx

● ACTUAL SIZE

Windpipe (trachea)

Cartilage ring

Sneezing

Hiccuping

Laughing

Coughing

Mouth and throat

Food is essential for life. It provides the energy needed for all the body's activities. It enables children to grow into adults. It repairs parts of the body as they wear out. And it provides an insulating layer that keeps you warm. Before food can do any of these jobs, however, it has to be changed into a form the body can use. This task is carried out by the digestive system, essentially a long tube, up to 29 feet (9 m) long, that runs from mouth to anus. As food passes along the digestive system, it is broken down into smaller and simpler pieces. The food can now be absorbed into the bloodstream and used by the body.

Food enters the digestive system through the mouth and throat. Inside the mouth, food is bitten and crushed in preparation for its journey down the throat.

PROCESSING FOOD
Seeing chewed-up food in someone's mouth is not very pleasant. However, it highlights how food changes between plate and throat. Different parts of the mouth have different roles in this process. Teeth grab food, then chop, tear, and grind it into small pieces. The strong, muscular tongue crushes and mixes the food. Salivary glands squirt saliva into the mouth, wetting the food and making it slimy enough to swallow. Lips stop the food from falling out.

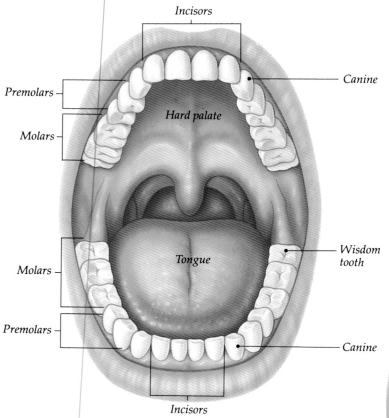

Incisors
Canine
Premolars
Hard palate
Molars
Molars
Tongue
Wisdom tooth
Premolars
Canine
Incisors

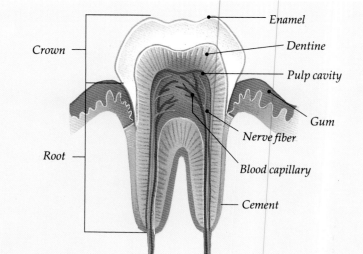

Crown
Enamel
Dentine
Pulp cavity
Gum
Nerve fiber
Root
Blood capillary
Cement

INSIDE A TOOTH
Teeth are tough. They have to be in order to withstand years of biting, crushing, and grinding. By cutting a tooth in half, you can see where its toughness comes from. Its crown is covered by enamel, the hardest material in the entire body. To stop it falling out, this molar's root is held firmly in its socket by "cement."

TYPES OF TEETH
Teeth come in various shapes and sizes. The flat ones at the front are called incisors. They chop food into chunks small enough to fit into your mouth. Next to them are the more pointed canines that grip and tear food when you are biting something tough. Now come the premolars and molars. Broad and flat, they crush and grind food into tiny pieces for swallowing. Do you have the same number of teeth as the picture above?

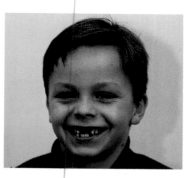

SETS OF TEETH
Babies' first teeth, the milk teeth, appear at six months. By the age of two, a child has a full set of 20. Below them, a second set of permanent teeth is growing. As these erupt from the jaw, the milk teeth fall out. There are 32 permanent teeth – the last four of these, the "wisdom" teeth, may not arrive until the age of twenty, if at all.

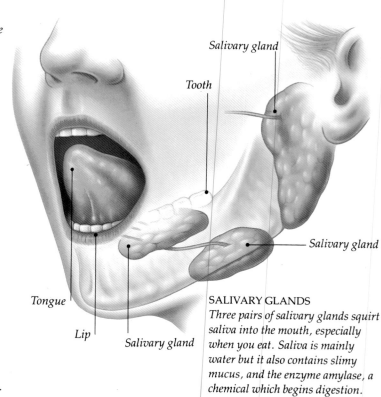

Salivary gland
Tooth
Tongue
Lip
Salivary gland
Salivary gland

SALIVARY GLANDS
Three pairs of salivary glands squirt saliva into the mouth, especially when you eat. Saliva is mainly water but it also contains slimy mucus, and the enzyme amylase, a chemical which begins digestion.

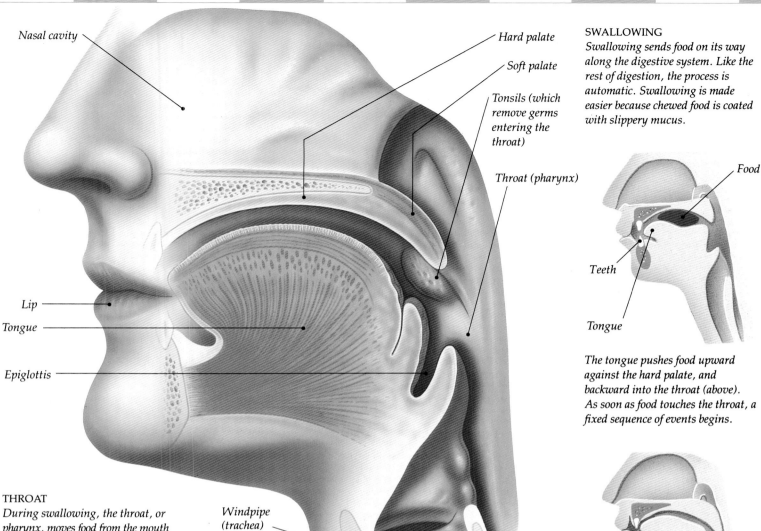

Nasal cavity

Hard palate

Soft palate

Tonsils (which remove germs entering the throat)

Throat (pharynx)

Lip

Tongue

Epiglottis

Windpipe (trachea)

● ACTUAL SIZE

Esophagus

THROAT

During swallowing, the throat, or pharynx, moves food from the mouth to the esophagus. The pharynx runs from where your mouth and nasal cavity meet, to the point where the windpipe and esophagus split. Around 5 inches (13cm) long, the throat looks a bit like a red garden hose. Its entrance is protected by tonsils. They pick up any harmful germs that come in with food, or in the air stream, and destroy them. If you look in a mirror, you can see that your throat is moist and glistening. This is because it produces mucus which makes sure that food slides down it easily.

SWALLOWING

Swallowing sends food on its way along the digestive system. Like the rest of digestion, the process is automatic. Swallowing is made easier because chewed food is coated with slippery mucus.

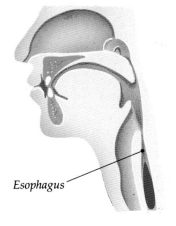

Food

Teeth

Tongue

The tongue pushes food upward against the hard palate, and backward into the throat (above). As soon as food touches the throat, a fixed sequence of events begins.

Epiglottis

As throat muscles squeeze food downward, the lidlike epiglottis closes the entrance to the windpipe. This stops food "going down the wrong way" into the lungs and choking the eater.

Carbohydrate-rich foods

Protein-rich foods

Fat-rich foods

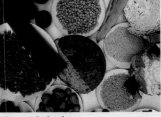

Fiber-rich foods

HEALTHY DIET

Your diet, the food you eat every day, must include a mixture of foods to be healthy. This mixture should provide seven nutrients in balanced amounts. Three of these nutrients – proteins, carbohydrates and fats – are needed in quite large amounts. The body needs proteins in order to grow and repair itself. Carbohydrates provide energy, as do fats. Fats also help keep you warm. Fiber, vitamins, and minerals are needed in smaller amounts. Fiber is not digested, but it helps the digestive system work properly. Vitamins and minerals ensure that body cells work properly. The seventh nutrient is water.

Esophagus

Once food enters the esophagus, muscle contractions push it to the stomach. These waves are called peristalsis. Travel from throat to stomach takes around five seconds.

Stomach and liver

Your stomach and liver are not connected to each other, but sit together in the body. Both of them are involved in digestion.

Your stomach is a part of the long digestive tube running from your mouth to your anus. It is an enlarged area, shaped like a "J," with muscular walls. Its job is to store food and process it. Empty, your stomach has a volume of about 1/5 of a cup (50 ml), but it can expand to hold over 8 cups (2 l) of food after a big meal. Receptors in the stomach wall detect the wall stretching and tell your brain that you are full. Food generally remains in the stomach for around four hours, although fatty foods stay in the stomach longer. This explains why you feel full longer after eating fries than after eating bread.

Your liver processes recently digested food when it arrives in the blood from the small intestine (see pages 32–33). It also makes a liquid called bile that is squirted back into the small intestine where it helps digest the fatty food that the stomach has so much trouble processing. The liver is dark and red because of the large amounts of blood passing through it.

WHERE ARE THE STOMACH AND LIVER?
Both stomach and liver are found in the abdomen, just below the chest. The stomach lies on the left side, nearly hidden by the liver. The liver occupies more space on the right of the abdomen than the left.

STOMACH ENZYMES
Digestion is impossible without enzymes. These chemical digesters turn complex food molecules into simpler ones, which can be absorbed into the blood. The stomach produces two enzymes, pepsin and rennin. Pepsin breaks down proteins into simpler polypeptides. Rennin, produced only in young children, makes milk lumpy, so it stays in the stomach long enough to be digested.

Pyloric sphincter

Duodenum – first part of small intestine

● ACTUAL SIZE

HOW THE LIVER WORKS
The liver performs over 500 functions, most of which involve regulating what should be in the blood, and removing what should not be. One major function is to process food arriving from the small intestine, storing some, converting some, and allowing the rest to travel to where it is needed. It removes poisons and drugs from the blood. It makes bile used to help digest fat in the small intestine. And the heat the liver generates doing all this work helps keep the body warm.

Hepatic vein – carries "processed" blood from the liver

Liver

Portal vein – carries food-rich blood from the small intestine to the liver

Bile duct – carries bile produced in the liver to the small intestine

Hepatic artery – carries oxygen-rich blood into the liver

Gall bladder – stores bile until it is needed

Diaphragm

Right lobe of liver

Left lobe of liver

Falciform ligament

Esophagus —

Cardiac sphincter —

Body of stomach —

INSIDE THE STOMACH
The inside of an empty stomach is slimy because its lining is coated with mucus. And it is hilly because of the folds in its lining that allow the stomach to enlarge after a meal. There are sphincter muscles at the top and bottom of the stomach. These muscular rings, when contracted, stop anything flowing through them. The pyloric sphincter at the bottom is very strong. It keeps food in the stomach until it is completely liquidized. The cardiac sphincter at the top is weaker. It stops food from going back up to your mouth.

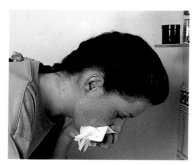

BEING SICK
Usually you vomit to rid your body of something disagreeable. The muscles of the abdomen contract, squeezing the stomach's contents up the esophagus and out of your mouth.

HEARTBURN
This chest pain, due to overeating, has nothing to do with the heart. It's caused by the stomach acid leaking into the esophagus and burning its lining.

— Wall of stomach

GASTRIC PITS
Millions of microscopic holes called gastric pits cover the stomach's lining. These pits produce mucus, acid, and enzymes. The thick mucus coats the stomach lining and stops it from being burned by the acid. The acid provides the right environment for the enzymes. And the enzymes digest the food.

STOMACH CHURNING
Food arrives in the stomach in the form of chunks. By the time it leaves, some four hours later, it resembles thick, creamy soup. What happens in between?

Well, the stomach is not just a rest area on the journey from mouth to anus. Its wall contains three layers of muscles that run around, along, and across the stomach. Their combined action twists, kneads, pummels, and crushes the food, and mixes it with digestive gastric juice.

At the same time, the muscles push the food mixture toward the pyloric end of the stomach, the exit point to the small intestine. Here, liquid food is squeezed into the intestine and any lumps are recycled for further crushing.

About five seconds after swallowing, a slimy ball of food, called a bolus, drops into the stomach, which is already starting to expand.

After two hours of kneading and crushing by stomach muscles, and digestion by gastric juice, food has been liquidized into a form that is called chyme.

After six hours, stomach muscles squeeze squirts of chyme through a slightly opened pyloric sphincter. The stomach starts to deflate — unless you have eaten again.

Food arrives in stomach

Stomach kneads food

Chyme squirted through pyloric sphincter

Intestines

The small and large intestines form the last and longest part of the digestive system, where as much goodness as possible is extracted from the food you eat. The intestines are surrounded by layers of smooth muscle that contract slowly and rhythmically, pushing the food along as it is digested and absorbed.

By the time food enters the small intestine from the stomach, it has been in the body for around four hours. As it passes through the small intestine, from duodenum to jejunum to ileum, it is bombarded with digestive chemicals called enzymes which break the food down into smaller and smaller particles. Now they are small enough to slip through the intestinal wall and into the blood transport system, where they are carried around your body. Anything that cannot be digested is squeezed into the large intestine and ready to be removed from the body.

WHERE ARE THE INTESTINES?
The small and large intestines take up most of the space in the abdomen. The abdomen is between the chest and hips.

HOW LONG?
Together the small and large intestines are over 20 feet (6 m) long. The small intestine is 16½ feet (5 m) long and the large intestine is 5 feet (1.5 m) long. To fit into the small space available, they are coiled up around each other.

INSIDE THE INTESTINES
Food undergoes dramatic changes as it travels along the winding, dark intestinal tunnel. In the small intestine, food is digested chemically, then absorbed. The digestion is done by enzymes, which break down large food particles into small ones. Tiny particles are absorbed through the wall of the small intestine into the blood. The blood carries it to every part of the body, where it can be used to produce energy or growth. Any food that cannot be digested passes on into the large intestine. Here all waste material is dried out before being pushed out through the anus.

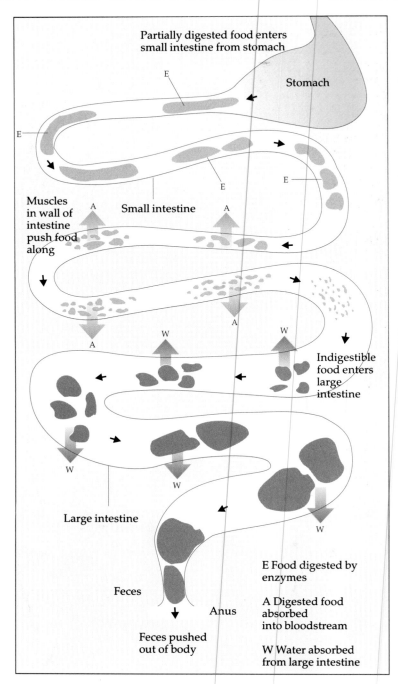

Partially digested food enters small intestine from stomach

Stomach

Muscles in wall of intestine push food along

Small intestine

Indigestible food enters large intestine

Large intestine

Feces

Anus

Feces pushed out of body

E Food digested by enzymes

A Digested food absorbed into bloodstream

W Water absorbed from large intestine

5m

HOW WIDE?
If the small intestine is so much longer than the large intestine, why is it called the small intestine? The reason is that the "large" and "small" refer to the width rather than the length.

● ACTUAL SIZE

Large intestine

Small intestine

The component parts of the large intestine – the colon and rectum – are wider than the component parts of the small intestine – the duodenum, the jejunum, and the ileum. The large intestine is 2½ inches (6.5 cm) wide, while the small intestine is just 1 in (2.5 cm) wide.

INSIDE THE SMALL INTESTINE
If you were small enough to walk along the inside of the small intestine, you would find yourself in a landscape of hills and valleys. The lining of the small intestine is a series of folds. Emerging from each fold are hundreds of tiny "fingers" called villi. The folds and villi provide a massive area for absorbing food. In fact, if all the folds and villi could be flattened out, the inner surface of the small intestine would be the same as the floor space of a two story town house.

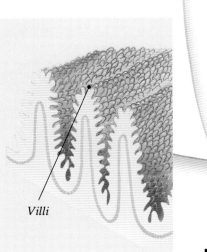

Villi

● ACTUAL SIZE

Esophagus

FOOD IN . . .
Food entering the intestine has already been churned and pounded by the muscles of the stomach for around four hours. Partially digested, the food is squirted into the duodenum, the first section of the small intestine. Called chyme, the food now resembles thick, creamy soup and is highly acidic. As soon as it enters the duodenum, the chyme is blended with juices from the pancreas and bile from the liver. These make the chyme less acidic. The pancreatic juice also contains some of the enzymes that will digest the food as it travels along the small intestine. Other enzymes are produced by the small intestine itself. The process of digestion and absorption will continue for twenty hours.

Duodenum

Stomach

Large intestine

Jejunum

Small intestine

Appendix

Ileum

APPENDIX
Where the small and large intestines join, there is a short tube that leads nowhere. This is called the appendix or, more properly, the vermiform (wormlike) appendix. The human appendix is rather mysterious. It plays no part in digestion or any other process. However, it is important and larger in animals that eat grass. Occasionally, the appendix becomes infected and inflamed, a condition called appendicitis. If this happens, it has to be removed by a surgeon.

Rectum

. . . WASTE OUT
Twenty four hours after being eaten, all that remains of a meal is food that cannot be digested. This might include materials such as plant fibers, better known as roughage. Mixed in with it are bacteria and dead cells scraped off from the inside of the intestine. Bile pigments from the liver provide a brownish color. This mixture is molded into moist feces, stored in the rectum, and pushed out when you go to the toilet.

Anus

Waste disposal

Several times a day, you stop whatever you are doing to urinate. The urine you pass out of your body is the product of a process of waste disposal carried out by your urinary system.

Wastes are produced by the chemical processes taking place inside all the body's cells. If they were allowed to build up, these wastes would poison you. Instead, they are filtered out of the blood as it travels through the kidneys. But the kidneys do more than simply remove wastes. They control the amount of water and salts inside the body. If you drink lots of water, or eat salty food, the kidneys will remove the excess.

Urine consists of filtered wastes, along with excess water and salts. Forty-seven gallons (180 l) of liquid is filtered out of the 450 gallons (1,700 l) of blood that flows through the kidneys each day. Most is absorbed back into the body, otherwise you would rapidly shrivel up due to water loss. Less than half a gallon (1.5 l) a day is discharged as urine. This trickles down the ureters into the bladder. When the bladder is full, it sends a message to your brain.

WHERE ARE THE KIDNEYS?
Your urinary system runs from the kidneys, which lie behind the liver and stomach, down the ureters to the bladder, and out through the urethra.

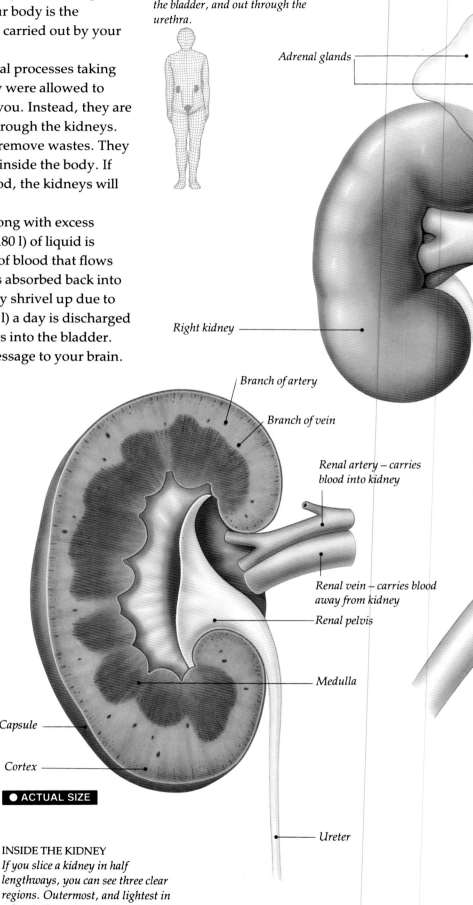

Adrenal glands

Right kidney

Branch of artery

Branch of vein

Renal artery – carries blood into kidney

Renal vein – carries blood away from kidney

Renal pelvis

Medulla

Capsule

Cortex

● ACTUAL SIZE

Ureter

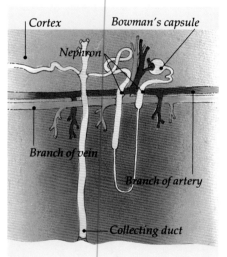

Cortex

Nephron

Bowman's capsule

Branch of vein

Branch of artery

Collecting duct

FILTRATION UNITS
Blood is cleaned in millions of tiny filtration units called nephrons that travel in twists and turns between cortex and medulla. Liquid is forced out of the blood as it passes through the knot of capillaries inside the hollow, cup-shaped Bowman's capsule. This filtered liquid contains not only water and waste, but also useful substances, such as glucose, which the body cannot afford to lose. As the liquid moves along the coiled nephron, most water and all the useful substances are taken back into the bloodstream. What remains – a mixture of water and waste – is called urine. Concentrated in the collecting duct, the urine drains into the renal pelvis and ureter.

INSIDE THE KIDNEY
If you slice a kidney in half lengthways, you can see three clear regions. Outermost, and lightest in color, is the cortex. Inside this, the darker, redder medulla is divided up into cone-shaped chunks called pyramids. In the center is the hollow, funnel-shaped renal pelvis, which runs into the ureter.

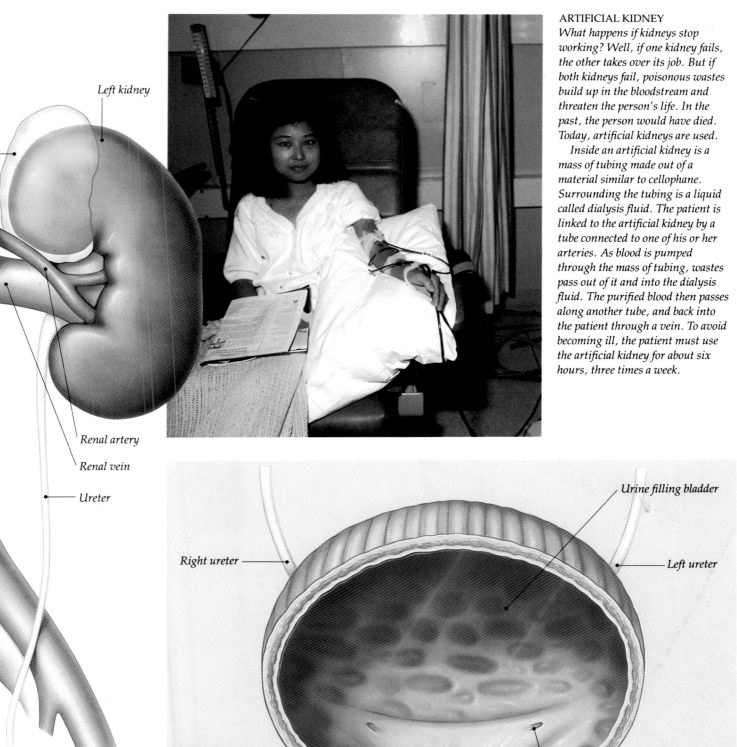

Left kidney

Renal artery

Renal vein

Ureter

Bladder

ARTIFICIAL KIDNEY
What happens if kidneys stop working? Well, if one kidney fails, the other takes over its job. But if both kidneys fail, poisonous wastes build up in the bloodstream and threaten the person's life. In the past, the person would have died. Today, artificial kidneys are used.

Inside an artificial kidney is a mass of tubing made out of a material similar to cellophane. Surrounding the tubing is a liquid called dialysis fluid. The patient is linked to the artificial kidney by a tube connected to one of his or her arteries. As blood is pumped through the mass of tubing, wastes pass out of it and into the dialysis fluid. The purified blood then passes along another tube, and back into the patient through a vein. To avoid becoming ill, the patient must use the artificial kidney for about six hours, three times a week.

Right ureter

Urine filling bladder

Left ureter

Muscular wall of bladder

Opening of ureter inside bladder

Sphincter muscle

Urethra

HOW THE BLADDER WORKS
Your bladder is an elastic, muscular bag. It stores the urine that is made continuously in the kidneys. Urine is squirted into the bladder through the openings of the two ureters. The exit, through the urethra, is clamped shut by a ring of muscle called a sphincter.

The bladder is the size of a walnut when it is empty. It expands like a balloon as it fills with urine. When it contains about a third of a pint (150 ml) of urine,

receptors in the bladder wall detect the surface stretching and send a message to the brain. Then you feel the need to go to the toilet. However, the bladder can continue to fill until it contains over 1 pint (500 ml) – two soft drink cans full – of urine. By this time you are desperate to go. Then when you relax the sphincter muscle, the muscles in the bladder wall push inward, and the urine flows out.

Brain

Touch the side of your head. Just one inch from your fingertips, floating in a shockproof fluid, and protected by the bony skull, lies 3 pounds (1.5 kilograms) of soft, pink-gray tissue, wrinkled on the outside like a walnut. This is your brain.

Your brain is your body's control center. It enables you to think, touch, hear, see, smell, and taste. It stores your memories, emotions, and feelings. It lets you learn, understand, and have ideas. It coordinates and regulates all body functions, even when you sleep.

Look inside and all you will see is a mass of nerve cells. Although the brain makes up just 2 percent of the body's weight, these cells consume about 25 percent of the body's energy. Working together, they enable you to recognize over 10,000 faces. In fact, this lump of soft tissue has powers above and beyond any computer yet built.

HOW MANY CELLS?
You have over 10 billion nerve cells in your brain. This is an unimaginably large number, more than the number of stars in the Andromeda galaxy (above).

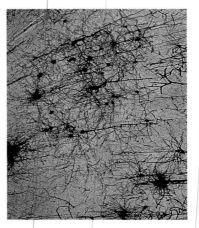

COMMUNICATION NETWORK
Between your 10 billion brain cells there are over 10 trillion connections. This network is not fixed, though. New connections are made all the time.

WHERE IS THE BRAIN?
Your brain is wrapped in three layers of membranes, and encased within the bony cranium. Here it floats in a sea of fluid, which protects it against accidental knocks.

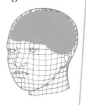

Your motor area sends instructions to your muscles, enabling you to move and balance. It also controls learned skills such as playing a musical instrument.

Your sensory area receives information from skin sensors all over the body. This is where you "feel" the outside world.

HOW THE BRAIN WORKS
The control center of your brain is the cerebral cortex. Some areas of the cortex receive and sort incoming messages from certain parts of the body. Others send out instructions.

Motor area

Thinking area

Sensory area

Hearing area

Sight area

The area at the front of your brain is the most complex part. It enables you to think, learn, plan, and have feelings and emotions. This is the home of your personality.

Your hearing area receives and interprets nerve impulses from your ears. It enables you to distinguish music from noise, thunder from a human voice.

Your sight area is where you see. Nerve impulses that travel from the eye along the optic nerve are turned into pictures here.

Right hemisphere of cerebrum

Corpus callosum – links right and left hemispheres

Pituitary gland

Brain stem

Cerebellum

● ACTUAL SIZE

Spinal cord

BETWEEN THE HEMISPHERES
The biggest part of your brain, the cerebrum, is divided into right and left halves, or hemispheres. Around the outside of each hemisphere is a folded layer about .13 inches (4 mm) thick called the cortex, or gray matter. This is the part of the brain that enables you to feel, think, remember, and act. By removing the left side of the brain, its other parts *can be seen. Nerve fibers in the corpus callosum link left and right hemispheres. The cerebellum enables you to balance, and move smoothly. The brain stem ensures that your heart and breathing rates match the body's activities.*

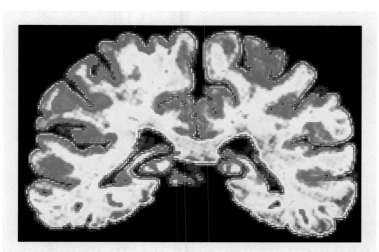

BRAIN SCANS
How can you look inside a brain to see what is wrong with it? In the past, the only way was to cut it open after its owner had died! Now doctors can look inside by using brain scans.

Brain tissue does not show up well on X rays. But when they are linked to a computer in a CAT (or Computerized Axial *Tomography) scan, the image of a thin "slice" through the patient's brain, or a 3-D image, can be built up.*

Doctors also use Positron Emission Tomography (PET) to examine the brain. A PET scan detects brain activity and shows which part of the brain is working at the time.

LEFT AND RIGHT BRAIN
Each side of your brain controls the actions of the opposite side of your body. Twiddle your left toe, and the instruction comes from the right side of the brain. Each side is also *involved with different skills. The right side of the brain deals with art and music; the left side of the brain deals with numbers, words, and problem solving.*

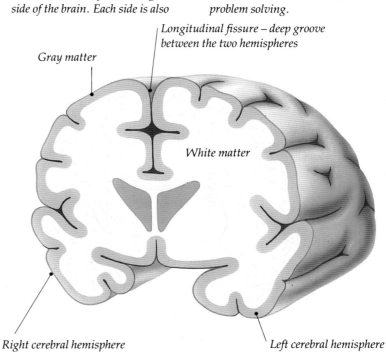

Gray matter

Longitudinal fissure – deep groove between the two hemispheres

White matter

Right cerebral hemisphere

Left cerebral hemisphere

Spinal cord and nerves

It is the nervous system that directly controls the body.
At its core are the brain and the spinal cord, which together
form the central nervous system (CNS). The brain is the
control center (see page 36–37), while the spinal cord links
the brain with the rest of the body and processes reflex
actions. Of course, the CNS cannot control the rest of the
body unless it is connected to it. This link is provided by
the nerves, which carry information in the form of
electrical impulses between the muscles and the sensory
organs and the CNS.

Right now, nerves are carrying impulses from your eyes
to your brain at a speed of about 250 miles (400 km) per
hour. While your brain interprets the words in front of you,
it sends out impulses to the eye muscles, instructing them
to move the eyes so you can read the rest of the line. And
these are just a few of the three million nerve impulses
speeding along the 47-mile (75-kilometer) network of nerves
each second.

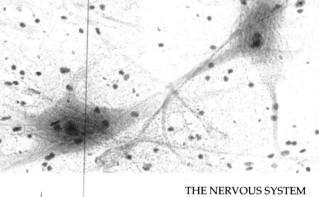

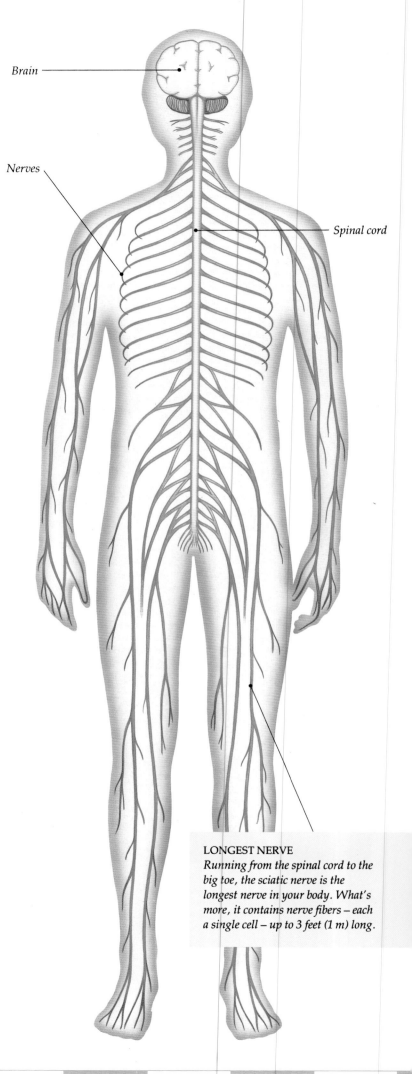

Brain

Nerves

Spinal cord

THE NERVOUS SYSTEM
*The brain, the spinal cord, and the
nerves that connect them to the rest
of the body make up the nervous
system. In it, each nerve cell (above)
communicates with many others to
form a massive control network.*

Nerve fiber

Connective tissue sheath
surrounding bundle of nerve fibers

Connective tissue sheath
surrounding nerve

INSIDE A NERVE
*Nerves consist of long nerve fibers
running parallel to each other in
bundles. These bundles are bound
together by a tough outer sheath.*

LONGEST NERVE
*Running from the spinal cord to the
big toe, the sciatic nerve is the
longest nerve in your body. What's
more, it contains nerve fibers – each
a single cell – up to 3 feet (1 m) long.*

Brain

Spinal nerve

Spinal cord

SPINAL CORD

As thick as a pencil, and about 18 inches (45 cm) long, your spinal cord runs down your back from the base of the brain. Surrounding and protecting the spinal cord is the backbone. Thirty-one pairs of nerves branch from the spinal cord, connecting it to every part of the body.

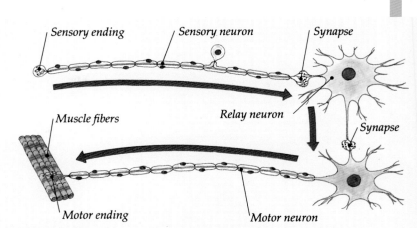

Sensory ending   Sensory neuron   Synapse

Relay neuron   Synapse

Muscle fibers

Motor ending   Motor neuron

HOW THE NERVES WORK

Nerve cells are called neurons. Their job is to carry electrical impulses and to pass them on to the next neuron. This happens across a gap called a synapse.

There are three types of neuron. When a sound receptor in your ear is stimulated, for example, it causes impulses to travel along a sensory neuron to the central nervous system (CNS). Here it passes its message on to a relay neuron which has links with many other neurons. These process the incoming information. Responding to the sound, the CNS may want to instruct a muscle to move. So the relay neuron passes the impulse on to a motor neuron, which carries it to a muscle.

Gray matter
White matter
Nerve rootlet
Spinal nerve
Protective membranes covering spinal cord

RAPID REFLEXES

This boy has just stepped on a pin. He immediately jerks his foot away from the offending object. This is a reflex action. Reflex actions are automatic responses by the body that help prevent it from being hurt. In this case, pain sensors in the foot detect the nail piercing the skin. Messages in the form of impulses rush along a sensory nerve to the spinal cord, and back along a motor nerve to a leg muscle that contracts, pulling the foot away. Reflex actions save valuable time because impulses short circuit through the spinal cord instead of traveling all the way to the brain for processing. A separate message is sent to the brain by a different route, causing the boy to say "ouch."

Skin

Your skin is a layer just .07 inches (2 mm) thick which, spread out, would cover an area of about 2½ square yards (2 sq m) – or thirteen times the area of the open book in front of you.

Skin is made of two layers. The outer epidermis replaces the dead cells that are constantly worn away from its surface. It also produces dark melanin that gives skin its color and protects skin cells from the harmful effects of the sun's ultraviolet rays. The inner dermis contains nerve endings that make the skin sensitive to heat, cold, pain, pressure, and touch. It also contains hair follicles that produce hairs, and sebaceous glands that make the oil that keeps the skin supple.

Skin forms a barrier against germ invasion. It stops water soaking into, or leaking out of the body. It helps you regulate body temperature. Skin is much more than a simple body covering!

Far from being flat, the skin's surface is scored by ridges and valleys, pitted with sweat pores, and has hairs sticking out of it like tiny tree trunks.

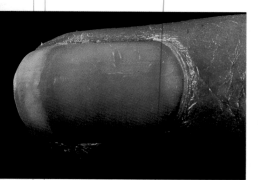

NAILS
Why doesn't it hurt when you cut your nails? Because, although they grow from living cells in the nail root, nails are dead. Like hair, nails are made of tough keratin. They protect the top surface of your fingertips and help you pick up objects. Fingernails grow about .02 inches (.5 mm) each week. They grow faster in warm weather and on the hand you use most.

FINGERPRINTS
Look at your fingertips. Each one has its own pattern of ridges that helps you grip objects, just as tire treads help a car grip a wet road. A thin layer of sticky sweat covers the fingertips, so that if you touch a hard surface you leave behind a fingerprint – a sweaty copy of the ridge pattern. The whorls and loops of a person's fingerprints are unique and easily identifiable. This is why they are so useful to the police. If they find clear fingerprints at the scene of a crime, they can be absolutely sure who made them.

The sweat pores in fingers may leave "poreprints" on a surface, too. These can also be used as evidence.

SKIN SENSITIVITY
The warmth of the summer sun. The shock of diving into an icy pond. The pain of a pinprick. The pressure felt when you shake hands. The soft texture of velvet. You experience all these sensations through your skin. Just below its surface are sensors that detect heat, cold, pain, pressure, and touch. They are not spread evenly over the body, however. Fingertips have more sensors than elbows, for example and feet more than knees. Hands and feet need to be specially sensitive because they are often our first point of contact with objects that may cut or burn.

Hair

Sensory ending – touch

Sensory ending – pain

Sensory ending – cold

Sensory ending – heat

Hair erector muscle

Sensory ending – pressure

HEAT SENSORS
You can confuse the heat sensors in your fingertips. Dip one finger in hot water and the other in cold, then dip both together in warm water. The "hot" finger will feel cold and the "cold" finger will feel hot.

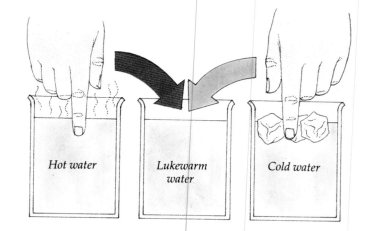

Hot water

Lukewarm water

Cold water

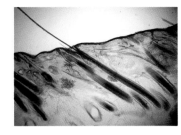

Your hairs are made of dead cells, reinforced with tough keratin, the material found in nails. Hairs are made by follicles. They spring from cells found at the bottom of deep holes in the skin.

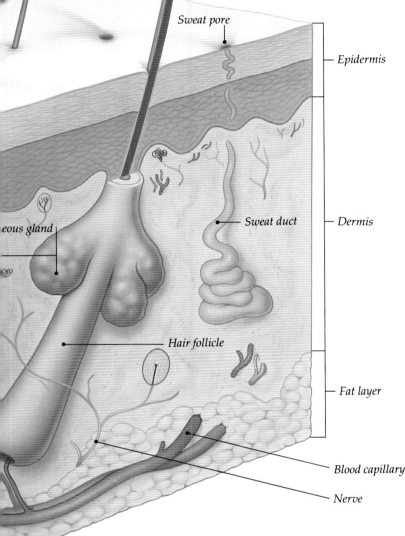

Sweat pore

Epidermis

eous gland

Sweat duct

Dermis

Hair follicle

Fat layer

Blood capillary

Nerve

HAIR TYPES

There are millions of hairs covering most of the body, apart from the lips, palms of the hands, and soles of the feet. These millions of hairs are divided into two main types: the fine hair that covers the bodies of women and children; and the longer, coarser hair found on everybody's head, and on the face and chest of men.

However, when people talk about hair, they usually mean the 100,000 or so hairs on the top of their head. These are either wavy, straight, or curly. The different types depend on the shape of the shaft of the hair. Wavy hair has an oval shaft. Straight hair has a round shaft. And curly hair has a flat shaft that looks like a ribbon.

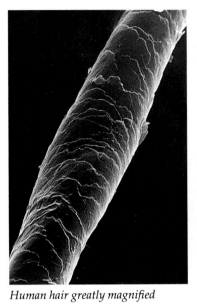

Human hair greatly magnified

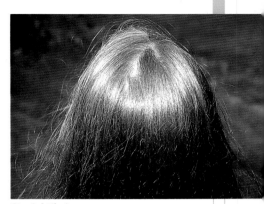

Straight hair

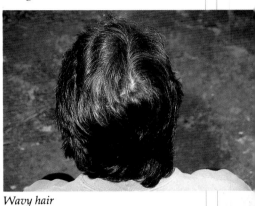

Wavy hair

Curly hair

SWEAT GLANDS

There are over 3 million sweat glands in your skin. Put end to end they would stretch over 6 miles (9.5 km). Each has a coiled-up part in the dermis that produces sweat, and a tube that carries sweat up to the skin's surface.

Sweat is mainly water with a dash of salt and waste. Usually you release about half a soda can-full each day, but this can increase to 2 pints (1 liter) a day in hot weather or if you exercise. Sweat helps you keep cool (see right).

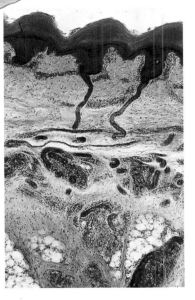

Cooling the body

Heating the body

TEMPERATURE CONTROL

Your body manages to keep its temperature remarkably constant – around 98.6°F (37°C) – whatever conditions are like outside. Temperature control is vitally important. If your body gets too hot, or too cold, it will not work properly and you may die.

Skin plays an important part in temperature control. If you are too hot, the blood vessels in the skin get wider and you look flushed. But because more blood is flowing, more heat is lost across the skin. The skin acts like a radiator cooling the body. At the same time, the sweat glands release lots of extra sweat onto the skin's surface. This evaporates, also cooling the body.

If you are too cold, blood vessels near the skin's surface get narrower. Your muscles contract, making you shiver, but releasing heat at the same time. Tiny muscles in the skin also pull on the body's hairs, giving you goose bumps.

Eyes

From the moment you are born, you depend on your eyes to provide you with a stream of information about shape, color and movement in the world around you. Most important of the sense organs, the eyes contain 70 percent of your body's sensory receptors. A million nerve fibers carry information from these receptors to the brain.

The eyeball is just 1 inch (2.5 cm) in diameter. Although a tough sclera – the white of the eye – covers most of it, the clear cornea at the front allows light in. This light is focused on the retina on the back of the eye, producing an upside-down image no bigger than a postage stamp. When the light hits the retina's sensory cells, they fire off messages, which are sent along the optic nerve to the brain. Here, in the visual area at the back of the brain, is where you actually see. In a tiny fraction of a second, the coded messages are unscrambled. The visual area of the brain also uses information from the muscles that move the eyes, along with visual clues from the outside, to enable you to judge distances accurately.

COLOR BLINDNESS

If you cannot see a number in this picture, you are one of the many males, and few females, who are color-blind. One of the three types of cones (see below) that recognize red, green or blue is missing from your retina, so you cannot distinguish certain colors.

WHERE ARE THE EYES?

Your two eyes are located in the front of the upper part of the head facing forward. Just one sixth of each eyeball is visible. The rest is cushioned by a pad of fat inside a protective bony orbit.

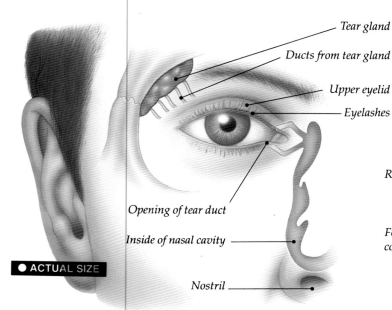

Tear gland

Ducts from tear gland

Upper eyelid

Eyelashes

Opening of tear duct

Inside of nasal cavity

● ACTUAL SIZE

Nostril

Upside-down image of kite projected onto retina.

Retina – light-sensitive layer

Fovea – dip in the retina where cones are concentrated

Blind spot – where optic nerve leaves eye

TEARS AND BLINKING

Generally, you only notice tears when you cry. In fact, you produce tears all the time. Tears form an essential part of the defense system that protects the front of the eye from dirt, dust, smoke, and germs carried in the air. They are made in the tear glands just above the eye, then spread over the front of the eye and moisten it. (Dry eyes feel very uncomfortable.) Tears also contain a chemical called lysozyme that kills germs.

Blinking helps spread tears over the eye. It is a reflex action and happens without you thinking about it, every three to seven seconds. The eyelids sweep tears and dirt into tiny holes in the corner of the eye. These empty into the tear duct, which is connected to the nose – which explains why you have to blow your nose when you cry. The blinking reflex also springs into action if something – an insect, say – suddenly approaches the eye, or if something touches the eyelashes, even a puff of air.

RODS AND CONES

In the retina, there are rod and cone cells that are sensitive to light. Your eye's 125 million skinny rods "see" in black and white only and work best in dim light. The 7 million dumpy cones "see" in color and work best in bright light. So in dim light you lose color vision.

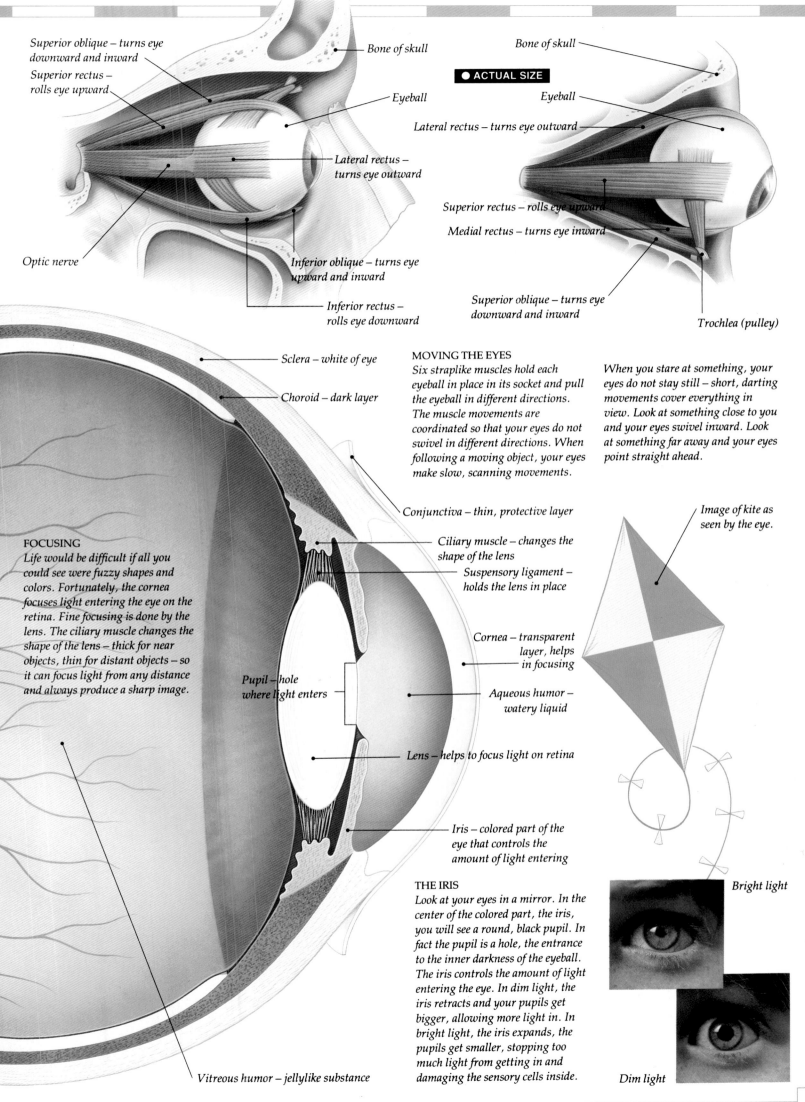

Superior oblique – turns eye downward and inward

Superior rectus – rolls eye upward

Bone of skull

Eyeball

Optic nerve

Lateral rectus – turns eye outward

Inferior oblique – turns eye upward and inward

Inferior rectus – rolls eye downward

Bone of skull

Eyeball

Lateral rectus – turns eye outward

Superior rectus – rolls eye upward

Medial rectus – turns eye inward

Superior oblique – turns eye downward and inward

Trochlea (pulley)

Sclera – white of eye

Choroid – dark layer

MOVING THE EYES
Six straplike muscles hold each eyeball in place in its socket and pull the eyeball in different directions. The muscle movements are coordinated so that your eyes do not swivel in different directions. When following a moving object, your eyes make slow, scanning movements.

When you stare at something, your eyes do not stay still – short, darting movements cover everything in view. Look at something close to you and your eyes swivel inward. Look at something far away and your eyes point straight ahead.

Conjunctiva – thin, protective layer

Ciliary muscle – changes the shape of the lens

Suspensory ligament – holds the lens in place

FOCUSING
Life would be difficult if all you could see were fuzzy shapes and colors. Fortunately, the cornea focuses light entering the eye on the retina. Fine focusing is done by the lens. The ciliary muscle changes the shape of the lens – thick for near objects, thin for distant objects – so it can focus light from any distance and always produce a sharp image.

Cornea – transparent layer, helps in focusing

Pupil – hole where light enters

Aqueous humor – watery liquid

Lens – helps to focus light on retina

Iris – colored part of the eye that controls the amount of light entering

Image of kite as seen by the eye.

THE IRIS
Look at your eyes in a mirror. In the center of the colored part, the iris, you will see a round, black pupil. In fact the pupil is a hole, the entrance to the inner darkness of the eyeball. The iris controls the amount of light entering the eye. In dim light, the iris retracts and your pupils get bigger, allowing more light in. In bright light, the iris expands, the pupils get smaller, stopping too much light from getting in and damaging the sensory cells inside.

Vitreous humor – jellylike substance

Bright light

Dim light

Ears

Sound is produced by a jumbo jet taking off, a crying baby, a classical sonata played on the piano, a whispered comment, and a breeze blowing through the leaves of a tree. Your ears enable you to hear all these sounds, whether they are soft or loud, pleasant or unpleasant, high-pitched or low-pitched. They allow you to appreciate the difference between a musical sound and raw noise, and between the voice of a stranger and the voice of a friend.

What most people familiarly call ears – the flaps that stick out from the side of the head – are in fact only a small part of the ear. They direct sound down a small tunnel, or canal, in the side of your head. The ear's inner workings are 1½ inches (4 cm) down that canal.

In the fluid-filled inner ear is the cochlea. This is shaped like a snail shell. Inside it are 20,000 sensory cells, each carrying 100 "hairs." When these "hairs" are bent by sounds transmitted through the ear, their sensory cells send nerve impulses to the brain. There, after the impulses are sorted out, you actually hear the sounds.

However, ears are more than just sound-detectors. Part of the inner region of the ear helps you balance by detecting the position of the head, and following its movements.

WHERE ARE THE EARS?
Your two ears are located on opposite sides of the head, just below the level of the eye. The ear canal secretes yellow-brown ear wax, (cerumen), which traps dust and insects. The ear is self-cleaning. The wax dries up and falls out of the ear. It is constantly being replaced.

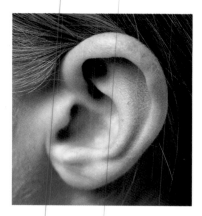

CATCHING SOUNDS
Sound waves are channeled into your ear by the shell-shaped pinna that surrounds the opening to the ear canal. Animals can move their ears to pinpoint sounds. You have to move your head to do that.

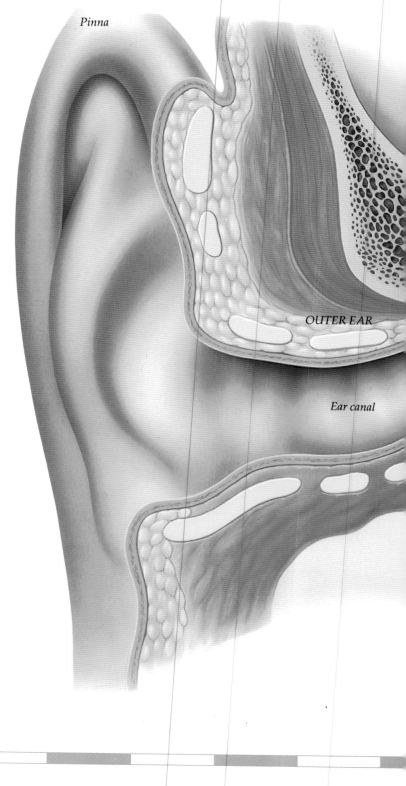

Pinna

OUTER EAR

Ear canal

SOUND DETECTION
Sounds travel through the air toward you in the form of waves, like the ripples produced when you toss a pebble into a pond. When sound waves traveling down the ear canal hit the eardrum, they make it vibrate. Fixed to the inside of the eardrum are the body's tiniest bones – the hammer, anvil, and stirrup, which are named for their shapes. As the eardrum vibrates, it moves the hammer. This causes the anvil to vibrate and push the stirrup. In turn, the stirrup is connected to the oval window, a membrane-covered hole guarding the entrance to the inner ear. As the stirrup moves in and out like a piston, it sets up vibrations in the fluid inside the cochlea. These vibrations bend tiny "hairs" on the end of sensory cells, causing them to send nerve impulses along the auditory nerve to the brain. Here the sounds are sorted out so that you hear them.

AIR PRESSURE
The Eustachian tube runs between the middle ear and the throat. It keeps air pressures equal on either side of the eardrum by allowing the eardrum to vibrate properly. By yawning or swallowing, you open the entrance to the tube. If air pressure changes suddenly, as it does when a plane takes off, swallowing helps you hear normally again.

If you could look behind the skin and bones covering the front of your face, you would see the delicate structures of the middle and inner ear just below, and behind, your eye.

BALANCING

Your ears play an important part in helping you balance. Next to the cochlea are three linked, C-shaped tubes called the semicircular canals. Like the cochlea, they are filled with fluid. In the bulges at the base of each canal, are sensory hairs embedded in jelly. When you move your head, the fluid inside the semicircular canals pushes the jelly, and bends the hairs, causing nerve impulses to be sent to the brain. Because the semicircular canals are set at right angles to each other, any head movement is bound to stimulate one or more canal. By

detecting which canals have been stimulated, the brain works out which way the head is moving. The utricle and saccule, next to the semicircular canals, also help you balance. They tell the brain whether you are upright, lying down, or standing on your head.

Other parts of the body also play a part in balance. Your brain receives a constant stream of information from pressure receptors in the soles of your feet, from your eyes, and from your muscles and joints to help it produce an up-to-date picture of the position you are in.

Saccule

Semicircular canals

Utricle

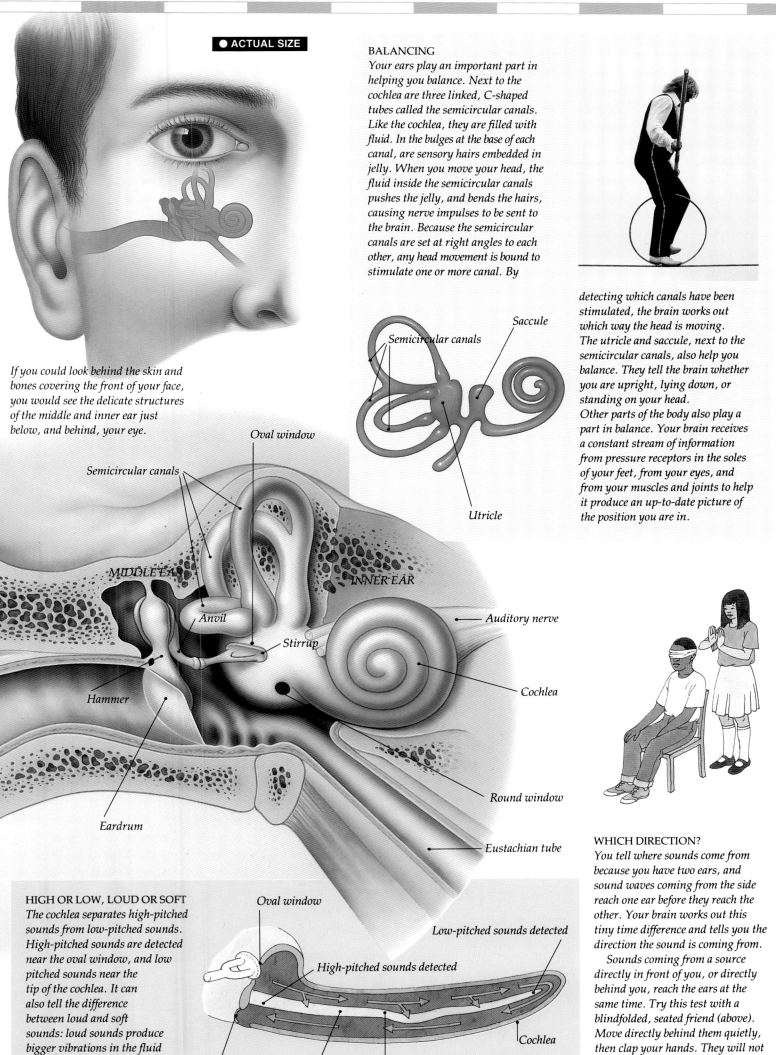

Oval window

Semicircular canals

MIDDLE EAR

INNER EAR

Anvil

Stirrup

Auditory nerve

Hammer

Cochlea

Eardrum

Round window

Eustachian tube

HIGH OR LOW, LOUD OR SOFT

The cochlea separates high-pitched sounds from low-pitched sounds. High-pitched sounds are detected near the oval window, and low pitched sounds near the tip of the cochlea. It can also tell the difference between loud and soft sounds: loud sounds produce bigger vibrations in the fluid inside the cochlea than soft sounds.

Oval window

Low-pitched sounds detected

High-pitched sounds detected

Cochlea

Round window   Hair cells   Medium-pitched sounds detected

WHICH DIRECTION?

You tell where sounds come from because you have two ears, and sound waves coming from the side reach one ear before they reach the other. Your brain works out this tiny time difference and tells you the direction the sound is coming from.

Sounds coming from a source directly in front of you, or directly behind you, reach the ears at the same time. Try this test with a blindfolded, seated friend (above). Move directly behind them quietly, then clap your hands. They will not be able to tell whether you are behind or in front of them.

Nose and tongue

How dull life would be if you could not smell a freshly opened rose or a home-cooked meal – or if onions and chilies, or pineapples and peaches, had no taste. Your senses of taste and smell – added to those of seeing, hearing, and touch – allow you to experience your surroundings fully.

Smell and taste are linked senses. Try this test. Blindfold a friend and give him or her small pieces of different foods to see if they can be identified. Now hold your friend's nose and repeat the experiment. Without a nose to help, it is much more difficult to identify what food you are tasting. The same thing happens when you have a bad cold and your nose is blocked.

Both nose and tongue are chemical detectors. Tiny particles that dissolve in the mucus lining the nose, or in saliva swilling over the tongue, are picked up by sensors that relay the information to the parts of the brain where you smell and taste.

WHERE ARE THE NOSE AND TONGUE?
Both tongue and nose are found inside the head. The actual "smelling" part of the nose is not in the fleshy part sticking out from the front of your face, but in the nasal cavity behind it. The muscular tongue is firmly attached to the bottom of the mouth.

SMELL VERSUS TASTE
Your sense of smell is at least 20,000 times more sensitive than your sense of taste. You can taste the bitterness of the flavoring quinine when it is diluted two million times in water, but you can smell skunk odor diluted 30 billion times in air!
And while your tongue can only detect four basic tastes, your nose can distinguish over 10,000 different odors.

INSIDE THE NOSE
Touch your nostrils with a finger and the back of your throat with your tongue. Between these two points lies the nasal cavity, the place where smelling happens. The nasal cavity has two sides, one for each nostril. At the top of each is a patch, no bigger than a postage stamp, covered with cells sensitive to odors. As air is breathed in, airborne particles come into contact with the patch, called the olfactory epithelium, and are detected.

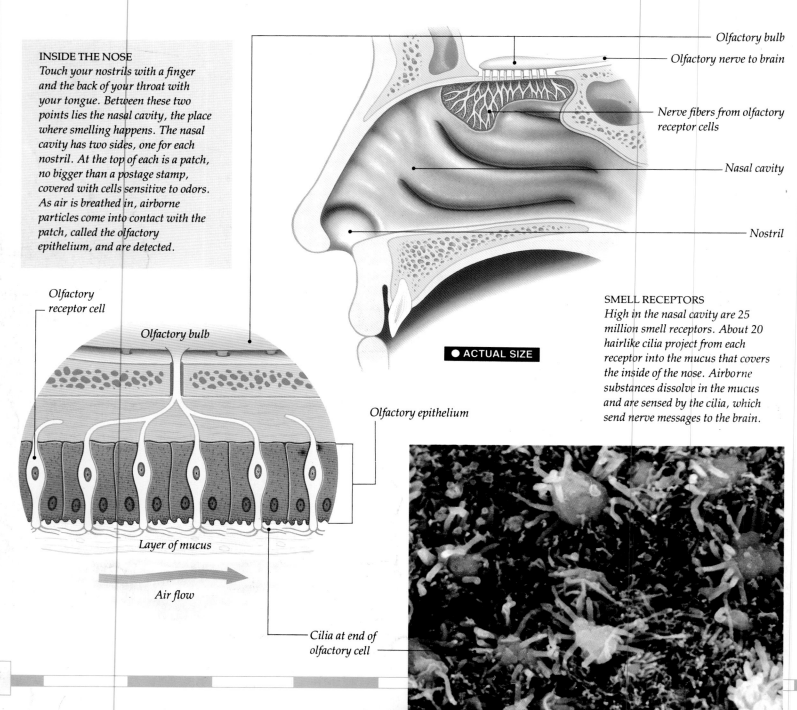

Olfactory bulb

Olfactory nerve to brain

Nerve fibers from olfactory receptor cells

Nasal cavity

Nostril

● ACTUAL SIZE

Olfactory epithelium

Olfactory receptor cell

Olfactory bulb

Layer of mucus

Air flow

Cilia at end of olfactory cell

SMELL RECEPTORS
High in the nasal cavity are 25 million smell receptors. About 20 hairlike cilia project from each receptor into the mucus that covers the inside of the nose. Airborne substances dissolve in the mucus and are sensed by the cilia, which send nerve messages to the brain.

TONGUE AND TASTING

Your tongue lets you savor and enjoy your food. At the same time, it guards the entrance to the digestive system, picking out anything that may be poisonous – which is usually bitter-tasting – so that you can spit it out before it does you harm. In fact, the tongue is 8,000 times more sensitive to bitter tastes than it is to the sweet tastes that are associated with harmless and nutritious things.

The tongue's taste detectors are 10,000 microscopic taste buds. Taste buds look the same but are not all sensitive to the same tastes. And they are grouped around the tongue

in different taste areas. You can see this on the taste map.

So how can you tell the difference between so many flavors when the tongue has only four basic taste sensations? Because the brain analyses how much of the four tastes is present. It adds to this information about the temperature, texture, and spiciness of food – along with the smells detected by the nose. So when you are presented with things as similar as raspberry and strawberry ice creams, for example, you are able to tell the difference without looking.

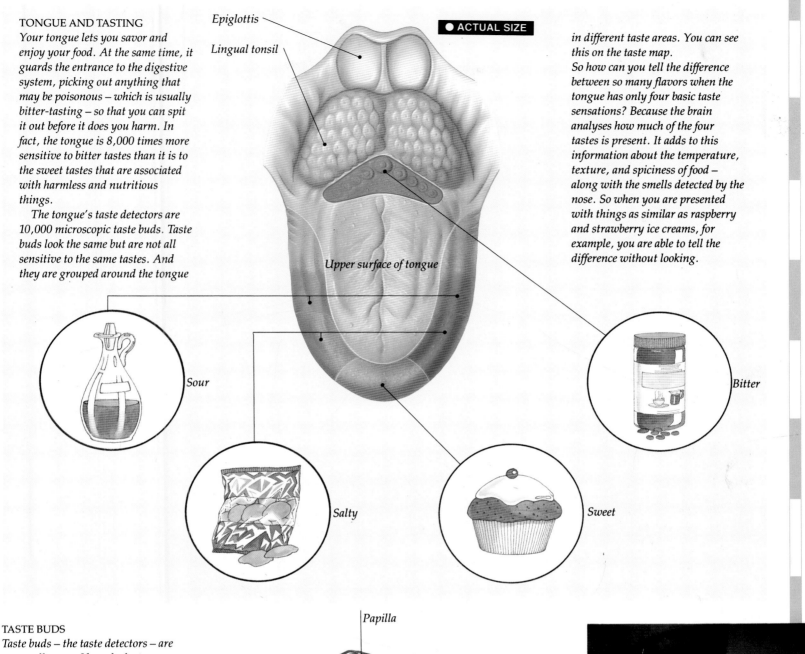

Epiglottis

Lingual tonsil

● ACTUAL SIZE

Upper surface of tongue

Sour

Salty

Bitter

Sweet

TASTE BUDS

Taste buds – the taste detectors – are too small to see. If you look at your tongue with a mirror, what you will see are hundreds of tiny bumps on the surface. These are called papillae, and make your tongue rough. The tiny taste buds line the gaps between papillae.

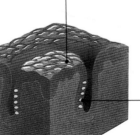

Papilla

Taste bud

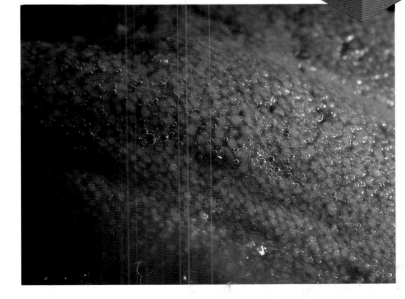

WINE TASTING

Some people's jobs depend on the fact that they can distinguish many more tastes than the rest of us. An example of this is wine tasting. Wine tasters do more than taste though. They depend on their sense of smell and their color vision as well. First, they examine the color of the wine. Then, they swill it around in the glass to release its smell, or "bouquet," which they sniff. Finally, a sip of wine is swirled over the tongue and tasted. By now the tasters can tell where the wine came from, how old it is, and whether it is any good.

Hormones

Consider the difference between telephoning friends for a quick chat and going around to see them for a meal. In the first case, communication is rapid and over quickly. In the second case, communication is achieved more slowly and lasts much longer.

The same comparison can be made between your nervous and hormonal (endocrine) systems. Both work together to coordinate the body's activities. But the nervous system does this instantly, by sending electrical impulses along the nerves, while the endocrine system takes a more leisurely approach. The endocrine glands that make up the system release over 20 kinds of chemical messengers called hormones into the bloodstream. These are carried to areas sensitive to the hormone, called target tissues, where they have a long-lasting effect.

Most endocrine glands are controlled by hormones released by the tiny pituitary gland, which is found at the base of the brain. In fact, the pituitary gland used to be called the "conductor of the endocrine orchestra," but it is now known that it is itself controlled by part of the brain called the hypothalamus.

WHERE ARE THE ENDOCRINE GLANDS?
You have six main endocrine glands in your body: one in the head; two (one of which has four parts) in the chest; and three (two of which are split into pairs) in the abdomen – in males one pair, the testes, hangs outside the body.

MALE   FEMALE

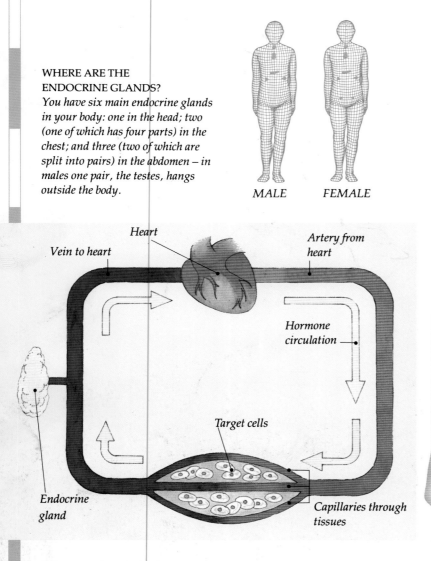

Heart

Vein to heart

Artery from heart

Hormone circulation

Target cells

Endocrine gland

Capillaries through tissues

HOW THE HORMONES WORK
A hormone has to carry its message from an endocrine gland, where it is made, to the target cells, where it has its effect. To do this, cells inside the gland release the hormone into a vein. It is then carried in the blood to the heart, which pumps it out to the tissues along an artery. The capillaries (see pages 20–21) then take the hormone to the target cells. And when it reaches the target cells, the hormone's molecules lock onto the surface and transmit their chemical instructions.

Pituitary gland

Thyroid and parathyroid

Adrenal glands

Pancreas

Ovaries

Testes (in man)

PITUITARY GLAND

No bigger than a garden pea, your pituitary is the most important gland of the hormonal system. It releases hormones that control growth, stimulate the thyroid gland, tell the breasts to produce milk, trigger the contraction of the womb when giving birth, control how much urine is produced, and tell the testes and ovaries to make sperm and eggs.

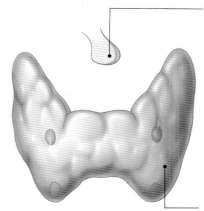

THYROID AND PARATHYROID

Your thyroid gland produces thyroxine. This controls the metabolic rate – the rate at which energy is released – of body cells. The four parathyroid glands release a hormone that controls levels of calcium in your bones and blood.

ADRENAL GLANDS

Each pyramid-shaped adrenal gland has two parts. The outer part makes over 24 hormones, including aldosterone, which controls salt levels in your blood. The inner part makes the fight-or-flight hormone, adrenaline (see right).

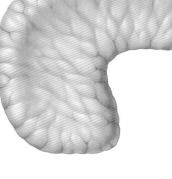

● ACTIVE SIZE

PANCREAS

Your pancreas produces two hormones, insulin and glucagon. Between them, they keep the level of glucose in the blood steady. Having too much, or too little, energy-providing glucose in the blood makes you very ill.

OVARIES

A woman's ovaries make the female sex hormones, estrogen and progesterone. Estrogen causes the development of female sexual features, such as breasts. Both hormones help regulate the menstrual cycle (see pages 52–53).

TESTES

A man's testes make the male sex hormone testosterone. Testosterone causes male sexual characteristics – such as a deeper voice, and facial and pubic hair – to develop and be maintained. Along with other hormones from the pituitary gland, testosterone stimulates the production of sperm by the testes.

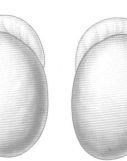

GROWTH HORMONE

As its name suggests, growth hormone makes the body grow. Growth hormone is produced by the pituitary gland and has most effect on bones and muscles making them grow longer. Its most dramatic effects can be seen during childhood and adolescence, the years when most growth takes place. Too little growth hormone during childhood causes a person to grow up to be shorter than normal. Too much growth hormone, and a person can grow to over 7 feet (2.1 m).

INSULIN

Insulin helps you keep a steady level of glucose in your blood by telling body cells how much glucose to take in from the blood after a meal. Without insulin, glucose levels would rise, eventually causing death. Diabetics – people who suffer from the disease diabetes – produce little or no insulin. They control their blood glucose by injecting insulin (left).

ADRENALINE

Adrenaline helps the body react if you are frightened. When you are scared, your brain sends a message to the adrenal glands, which release adrenaline into the blood. Immediately, your heart starts pounding, and you breathe more quickly. Your muscles get an increased supply of energy – providing food and oxygen so that you are ready to confront the danger – or, to run away.

Communication

Humans are the only animals that use spoken language to make themselves understood. The brain works out what you want to say, and then instructs the mouth, tongue, and lips to form the words. Language is very complex. It can be used to express facts, ideas, or any number of feelings. Yet when you are not speaking, you are still busy communicating in a number of nonverbal ways, that is without using words at all.

Facial expressions can say a lot about the way you feel about yourself, and the way you relate to someone else. A real smile, or a forced one, a frown, a pout, or a grin, all serve to convey something about a person.

Keeping eye contact is important, too. If you look into someone's eyes and they return your gaze, this generally shows that you are showing interest in each other. If you stare, you indicate hostility.

Simply turning toward, or away from, someone can say much more than words. Gestures, body positions, and movements make up the repertoire of nonverbal communication called body language.

BODY LANGUAGE
Body language is a way we communicate without words. A lot is said by the way someone holds their body, leans toward you or folds their arms. Your brain reacts to the position and movements of other people's bodies and extracts what the message of the body language might mean – perhaps this person likes you, or perhaps you bore them!

● ACTUAL SIZE

MAKING SOUNDS
Spoken language is a form of communication unique to humans. Your brain controls what you want to say and how you want to say it. It does this by sending messages to your larynx (voice box), tongue, and lips. The larynx produces the "raw" sounds by closing the vocal cords. These sounds are refined by the tongue to produce the "harder" consonant sounds such as "L" and "T." The production of vowel sounds – "A," "E," "I," "O," and "U" – is controlled by the shape of your lips.

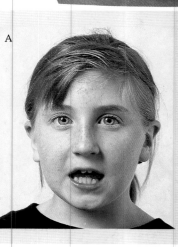

FACIAL MUSCLES

The muscles of your face overlay the bones of your skull, producing the features that make an individual recognizable and unique.

Frontalis – raises the eyebrows and wrinkles the forehead

Orbicularis oculi – causes blinking and squinting, and narrows the eyes

Zygomaticus – makes you smile

Risorius – makes you grin

Orbicularis oris – closes mouth and purses lips, as in kissing

Depressor labii inferioris makes you pout

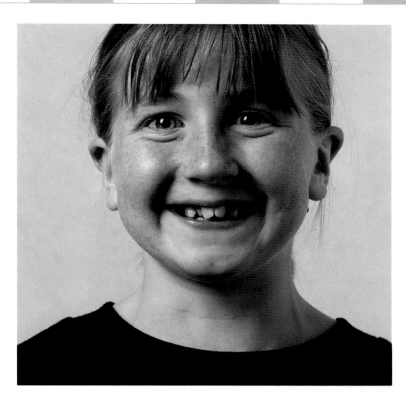

The muscles of the face, scalp, and neck pull on the skin. There are many of them and they can express a wide variety of emotions. Frowning takes more effort than smiling. You use 43 to frown but only 17 to smile.

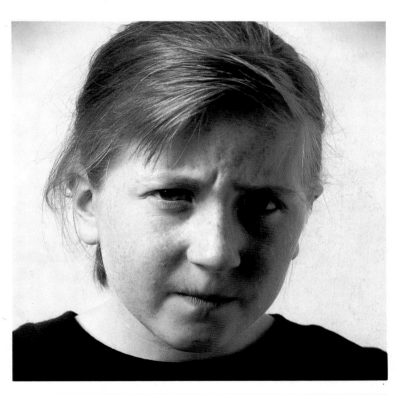

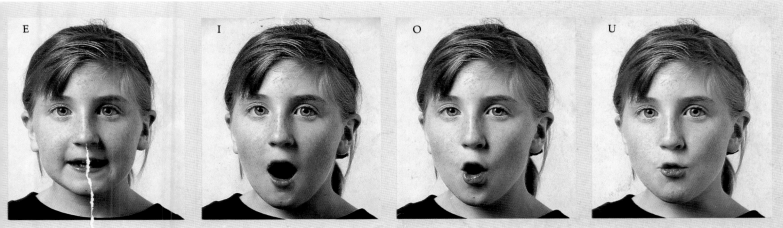

E   I   O   U

A new life

You began life as a single cell smaller than the full stop at the end of this sentence. That single cell was produced at fertilization, when chemical information from your father joined with chemical information from your mother. The result, a fertilized egg, carried all the instructions needed to make you.

Every day, millions of fertilizations take place. Each depends on an encounter between a sperm – one of the tiny tadpolelike cells produced in a man's testes – and an egg, a bigger cell released each month from a woman's ovary. These two elements are united in the fertilized egg cell, which then undergoes the first of many divisions and embeds itself in the soft wall of the uterus (womb). There the egg continues its development for the next nine months. During that time, the single cell becomes a mass of many billions of cells that make up a new human being.

AN EGG IS RELEASED

When a girl is born, her two ovaries contain about 700,000 immature eggs. Every month, from about the age of 12 to about the age of 50, one of these many eggs gets bigger. Then a small piece of the ovary wall splits open, and the egg is released from the ovary. This process is called ovulation. The egg is then wafted along the Fallopian tube toward the uterus. If the egg is fertilized (see below) by a sperm within the next 24 hours, it will grow into a baby in the uterus. If it is not fertilized, the egg and the lining of the uterus, which thickens to receive the fertilized egg, break down and pass out of the vagina. This is called menstruation, or having a period.

WHERE ARE THE REPRODUCTIVE ORGANS?

Most of the male reproductive system hangs outside, and toward the front of, the body, at the top of the legs. The penis and urethra also form part of the urinary system.

MALE

The female reproductive organs – the ovary, Fallopian tubes, uterus, and vagina are located in the lower part of the abdomen. The vagina opens between the legs.

FEMALE

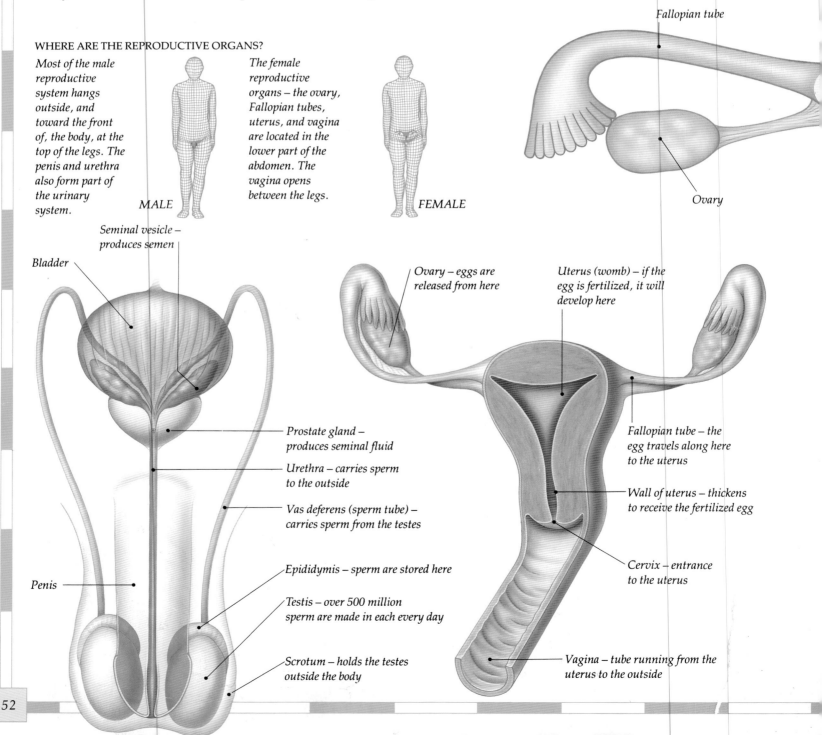

Fallopian tube

Ovary

Bladder

Seminal vesicle – produces semen

Penis

Prostate gland – produces seminal fluid

Urethra – carries sperm to the outside

Vas deferens (sperm tube) – carries sperm from the testes

Epididymis – sperm are stored here

Testis – over 500 million sperm are made in each every day

Scrotum – holds the testes outside the body

Ovary – eggs are released from here

Uterus (womb) – if the egg is fertilized, it will develop here

Fallopian tube – the egg travels along here to the uterus

Wall of uterus – thickens to receive the fertilized egg

Cervix – entrance to the uterus

Vagina – tube running from the uterus to the outside

SEXUAL INTERCOURSE

To start a new life, a sperm from the man's testes has to fertilize an egg in a woman's Fallopian tube. For this to happen, sexual intercourse, or "making love," has to take place. Sexual intercourse is a very intimate type of contact between two people. As the couple touch and caress each other, they become sexually excited. The woman's vagina moistens. The man's penis elongates and becomes stiff. The woman then takes the penis into her vagina, and they move together. At the height of excitement, a milky fluid called semen containing millions of sperm is squirted out of the penis and into the vagina. The sperm then begin their long journey up through the uterus and into the Fallopian tube. Here, if an egg is present, one of the few sperm that survive the journey will fertilize it.

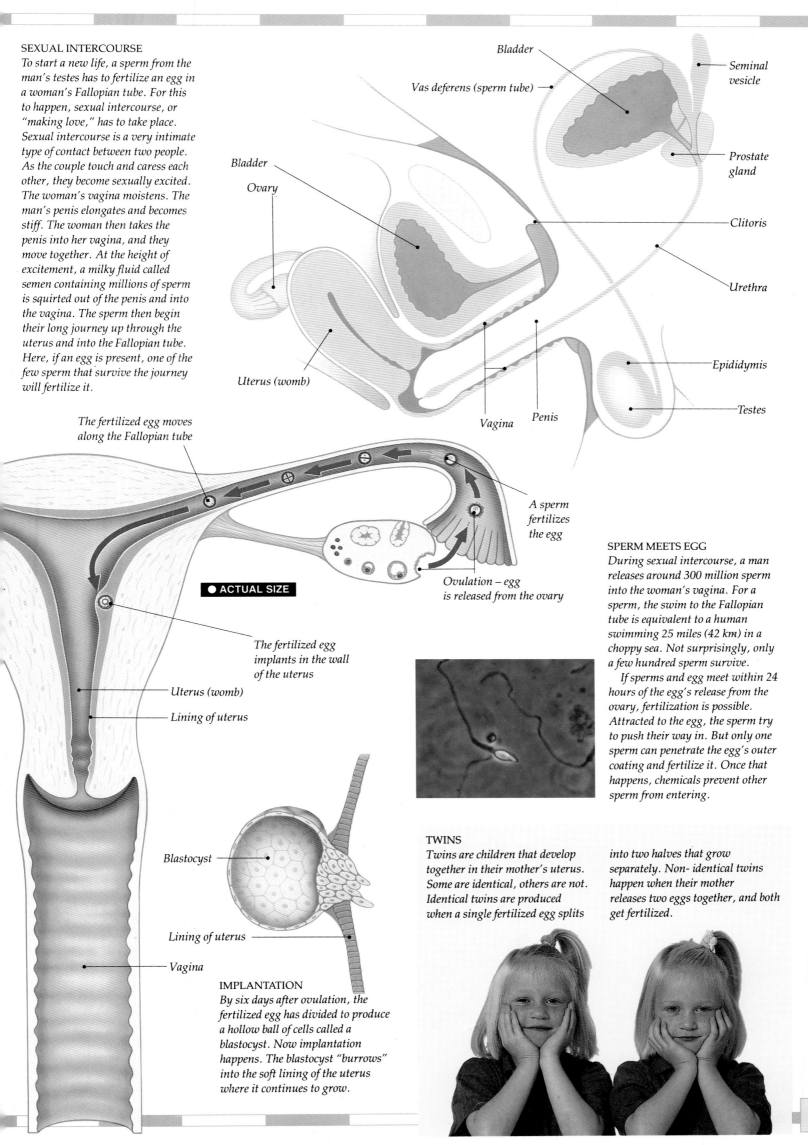

Bladder

Vas deferens (sperm tube)

Seminal vesicle

Prostate gland

Clitoris

Urethra

Epididymis

Testes

Bladder

Ovary

Uterus (womb)

Vagina

Penis

The fertilized egg moves along the Fallopian tube

A sperm fertilizes the egg

Ovulation – egg is released from the ovary

● ACTUAL SIZE

The fertilized egg implants in the wall of the uterus

Uterus (womb)

Lining of uterus

Blastocyst

Lining of uterus

Vagina

SPERM MEETS EGG

During sexual intercourse, a man releases around 300 million sperm into the woman's vagina. For a sperm, the swim to the Fallopian tube is equivalent to a human swimming 25 miles (42 km) in a choppy sea. Not surprisingly, only a few hundred sperm survive.

If sperms and egg meet within 24 hours of the egg's release from the ovary, fertilization is possible. Attracted to the egg, the sperm try to push their way in. But only one sperm can penetrate the egg's outer coating and fertilize it. Once that happens, chemicals prevent other sperm from entering.

IMPLANTATION

By six days after ovulation, the fertilized egg has divided to produce a hollow ball of cells called a blastocyst. Now implantation happens. The blastocyst "burrows" into the soft lining of the uterus where it continues to grow.

TWINS

Twins are children that develop together in their mother's uterus. Some are identical, others are not. Identical twins are produced when a single fertilized egg splits into two halves that grow separately. Non- identical twins happen when their mother releases two eggs together, and both get fertilized.

In the womb

It takes nine months for the dot-sized fertilized egg to grow inside a mother's womb into a fully developed baby.

The fertilized egg divides repeatedly and grows into a tiny embryo. By five weeks, the heart is beating. By eight weeks, the embryo looks human and is now called a fetus. Day by day, during the following seven months, the fetus grows rapidly until, nine months after fertilization, it is ready to be born. Throughout its development, the fetus floats inside a protective bag of liquid, kept at a constant temperature inside the womb. Food and oxygen are carried to the fetus along the umbilical cord that links it to the mother.

MULTIPLYING CELLS

Thirty-six hours after a father's sperm meets a mother's egg at fertilization (see pages 52–53), the fertilized egg has moved farther toward the uterus, and has divided into two. By 72 hours, three more divisions have happened to produce a ball of 16 cells called a morula. By 144 hours, further cell divisions have produced a hollow ball of cells called a blastocyst which attaches itself to the wall of the uterus. Within eight weeks, this will be recognizable as a tiny human being.

Two cell stage – 1½ days after fertilization

Morula stage – 3 days after fertilization

Blastocyst stage – 6 days after fertilization

Embryo at 5 weeks
.3 inches (8 mm) long
The brain is developing quickly
Arm and leg buds appear
The beginning of the eye can be seen
The heart is beating

Fetus at 8 weeks
1.13 inches (3 cm) long
The main outside parts of the body are now formed: ears, eyes, mouth, arms, legs, fingers, and toes

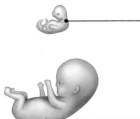

Fetus at 12 weeks
3.5 inches (9 cm) long
All the internal organs are formed
Sex can now be determined

Before pregnancy *16 weeks pregnant*

Fetus at 16 weeks
5.3 inches (14 cm) long
Faces looks human
Sucking movements of lips and blinking occur

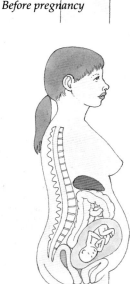

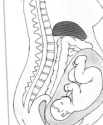

28 weeks pregnant *38 weeks pregnant*

Fetus at 20 weeks
7.25 inches (19 cm) long
Hair grows on the head and body
Kicking and hiccuping can be felt by the mother

THE GROWING UTERUS

Before pregnancy, the uterus is the size of a fist. By 16 weeks it fills the space inside the hips, and the mother's abdomen starts to bulge. By 28 weeks, it fills about half the abdomen, and by the end of pregnancy, at 38 weeks, the uterus fills most of the abdomen, right up to the ribs.

BABY'S LIFELINE

How does the growing fetus get supplies? Have a look at your "belly button" for the clue. This was where the umbilical cord was attached when you were in the uterus. This lifeline carries blood to and from the placenta. Here, mother and baby's blood systems come close enough for food and oxygen to be taken in from the mother's blood.

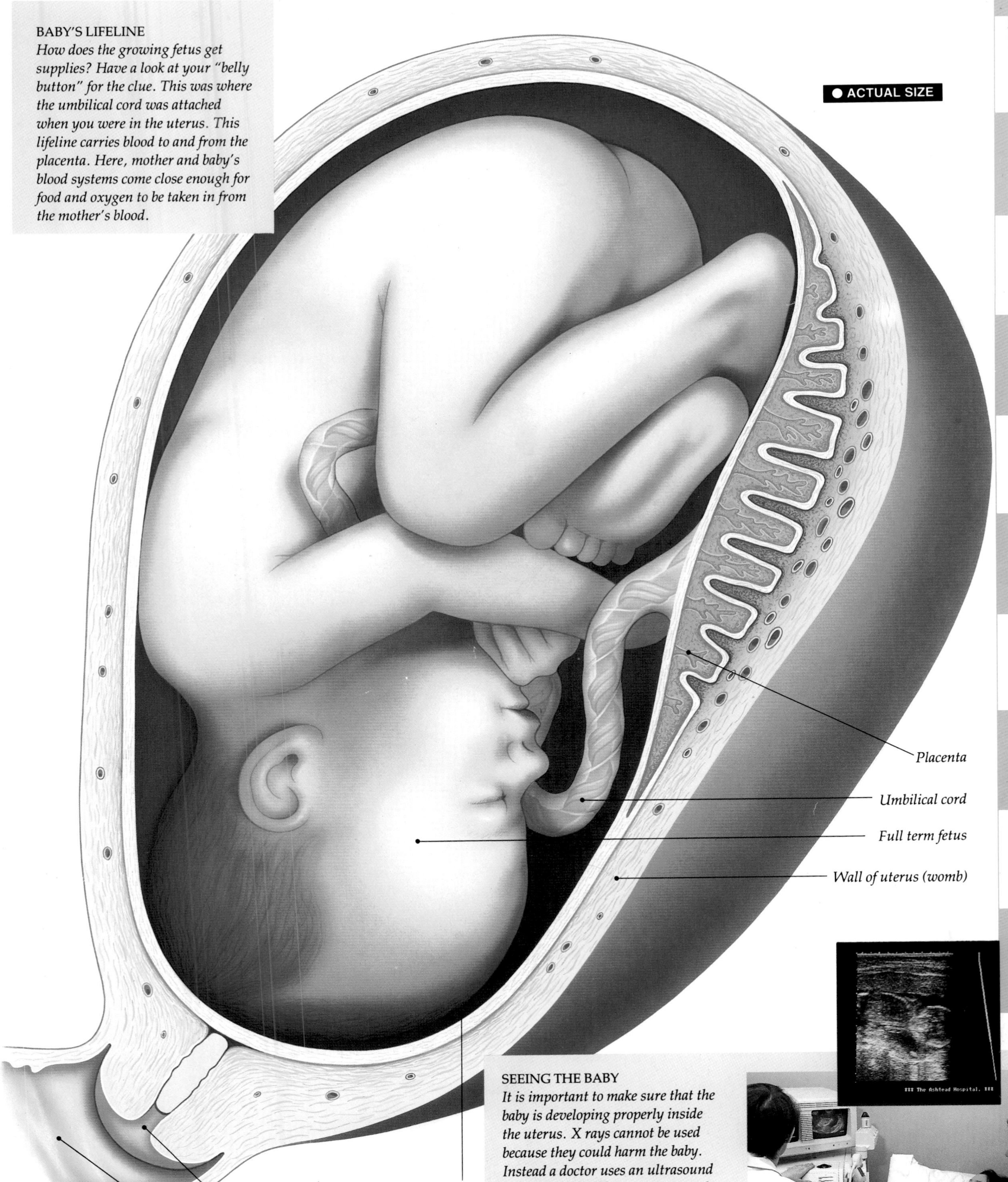
ACTUAL SIZE
Placenta
Umbilical cord
Full term fetus
Wall of uterus (womb)
Amniotic fluid – cushions and protects fetus
Cervix of uterus
Vagina
*** The Ashtead Hospital. ***

SEEING THE BABY

It is important to make sure that the baby is developing properly inside the uterus. X rays cannot be used because they could harm the baby. Instead a doctor uses an ultrasound scan (see right). A scanner, moved over the mother's abdomen, sends high-frequency sound waves into the uterus. These produce a "picture" of the baby that can be seen on a monitor by the side of the bed.

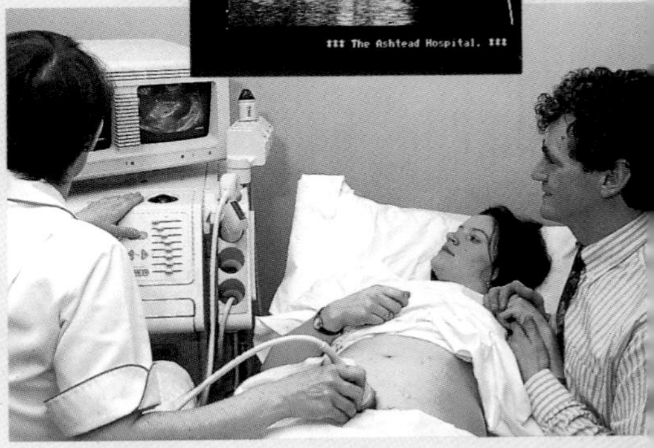

Birthday

About 266 days after fertilization, a baby is fully developed and ready to emerge into the outside world. The baby signals to its mother that it is ready to be born. She realizes the baby is on its way because of the pains she feels in her uterus, caused by the contractions of the muscles that will push the baby out of her body.

Birth can take anywhere between two hours and 24 hours or more. On average, babies weigh 7½ pounds (3.4 kg), and are about 20 inches (50 cm) long. When the baby appears, the first thing it does is to expand its lungs and start breathing. It is no longer cocooned within a safe, warm environment. Suddenly, it senses light and sounds around it, feels the air on its skin, and notices the change in temperature. It feels hungry and instinctively seeks out its mother's breast for its first feed. For the first few years the child needs constant attention. It will be years before it becomes independent.

BREAST-FEEDING

Many mothers breast-feed their babies for the first months of their lives. Breast milk is better for the baby than dried milk because it is fresh, free from germs, and contains the food the baby needs in the correct proportions.

For the first two or three days after birth, however, the breasts produce not milk, but a yellowish liquid called colostrum. This is rich in body-building proteins and disease-fighting antibodies. When true milk production starts, the baby's mother releases around two pints (1 liter) of bluish-white, quite sweet, milk each day. Sucking at the breast is an automatic, reflex action for the baby. It also stimulates the breasts to make more milk.

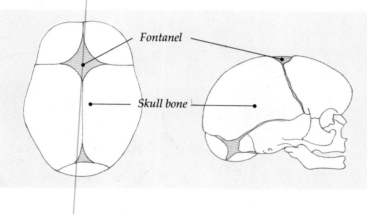

Fontanel

Skull bone

A FLEXIBLE SKULL

Your brain is surrounded and protected by a number of bones that are fused together to form a solid skull. But in a baby's skull, these bones are not fused together. The gaps between them are called fontanels. This makes the baby's skull slightly squashable – a useful feature when its head has to squeeze through the narrow gap in the center of its mother's pelvis and down the vagina.

THE STAGES OF LABOR

Labor is a series of events during which the baby is pushed out of its mother's uterus. When labor begins (1), the uterus starts to contract, weakly at first, then more strongly and more frequently. The cervix, the opening to the uterus, gets wider, and the bag of fluid surrounding the baby bursts – this is called "breaking water." This stage of labor can last for 12 hours, or even longer.

The uterus then starts contracting strongly every 2 or 3 minutes. The

uterus muscles push the baby's head out through the vagina (2). Once the head – the baby's widest part – has appeared, the rest of the body is delivered more easily (3). This stage takes between 20 and 50 minutes.

Once the baby is born and starts to breathe (4), the umbilical cord that links it to its mother is clamped and cut. About 30 minutes later, the placenta – now called the afterbirth – is delivered.

1. BEGINNING OF LABOR

2. HEAD ABOUT TO EMERGE

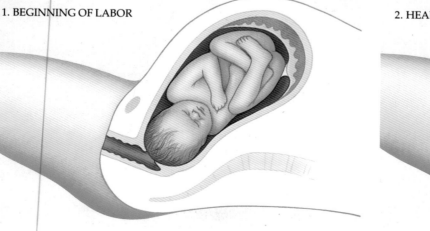

● ACTUAL SIZE

Clamp on cut
umbilical cord

A NEWBORN BABY

Being born is quite a shock for a baby! Imagine how you would feel if you were dragged out of a nice, warm room with plenty to eat and left somewhere cold, with no food or clothing. This is just what a baby experiences. One moment it is inside the uterus, floating in a dark, watery environment at constant temperature, with its food and oxygen provided. Then, suddenly, it is thrust out into a cold, light environment. Its life-support system is cut off so it has to breathe, eat, and excrete for itself.

Not only must the baby be fed regularly, but it must be kept warm because it cannot yet keep its own body temperature steady. All its needs have to be attended to by adults.

3. BABY IS BORN   **4. UMBILICAL CORD TIED AND CUT**

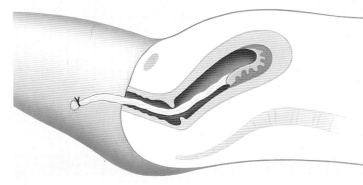

The growing body

Look at some photographs of yourself when you were a baby. The proportions of your body were different. As a baby, your head was about one-quarter the length of your body. By the time you are grown up, your head is only about one-eighth your body's length. The shape of your body also changes, especially around the age of 12 or 13.

Your body grows, changing in shape and size, through childhood right up to the age of 20. But it does not grow at the same rate during those years. Growth is very rapid during the first year of life. In middle childhood, the growth rate slows, then it suddenly increases again for the growth spurt that happens in girls between the ages of 10 and 14, and in boys between the ages of 12 and 16. This is the time of puberty, when the child's body matures and becomes adult.

After the age of 20, the body does not change much outwardly, although inside body cells are constantly being replaced. And in old age, growth is actually "reversed," and the body shrinks a little.

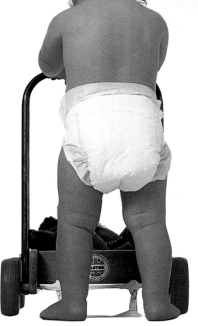

EARLY CHANGES IN THE BODY

Great changes happen to boys' and girls' bodies during the first year of life. Weight triples and height increases by a half. The brain grows from a quarter to half an adult size. The arms and legs grow faster as well, so that the head is no longer as large in proportion to the rest of the body. And the first teeth appear.

The first movements a baby makes are automatic reflex movements, such as grasping and sucking. Most have disappeared by the end of three months, as the baby starts to learn movements of its own. First, it learns to control its upper arms and legs, then its hands and feet, and finally its fingers. By nine months it can hold its head steady and crawl on its hands and knees. By the time it is one, the infant starts to walk and can pick up objects between fingers and thumb.

INFANT

6 months
The average height is 26 inches (.66 m), and average weight 16½ pounds (7.5 kg). Boys are slightly taller and heavier than girls. The baby can sit on a chair and reach for objects.

1 year
The average height is 2½ feet (.75 m), and average weight 22 pounds (10 kg). Boys are slightly taller and heavier than girls. The infant can pull itself up by holding onto furniture, and is learning to walk.

CHILD

6 years
The average height is 3 feet 10 inches (1.17 m), and average weight 47½ pounds (21.6 kg). Boys are slightly taller and heavier than girls. The child can walk and talk, read, and write.

8 years
The average height is 4 feet 3 inches (1.3 m), and average weight 59 pounds (26.8 kg). Boys are slightly heavier and taller than girls. The child's reading and writing powers have improved, and it can now ride a bicycle.

CHANGES DURING PUBERTY

Puberty marks the time when girls' and boys' bodies mature, at the end of childhood and the beginning of being an adult. The body grows rapidly and changes happen inside it that enable it to produce children of its own.

Puberty starts earlier in girls than boys, between the ages of 10 and 14, and lasts between two and a half to three years. As the girl's body gets taller and heavier, her hips widen and more fat accumulates under her skin, producing the more "rounded" shape of an adult woman. The girl's breasts grow and her nipples enlarge and stick out more.

Hair grows in her armpits and around her genitals. Her uterus and vagina enlarge and her ovaries start releasing eggs each month as menstruation begins.

In boys, puberty starts between the ages of 12 and 16 and takes around four years to complete. As his body gets heavier and taller, a boy's shoulders widen and his muscles thicken. Hair grows on his face, armpits and chest, and around his genitals. The boy's penis and testes get bigger, and the testes start producing sperm. His larynx (voice box) also enlarges, and his voice breaks and gets deeper.

ADOLESCENT

12 years
The average height is 4 feet 11 inches (1.5 m) for boys, and 5 feet (1.52 m) for girls. And average weight is 84 pounds (38.2 kg) for boys, and 88 pounds (40 kg) for girls. Girls are taller and heavier than boys because their puberty growth spurt starts earlier.

14 years
The average height is 5 feet 4 inches (1.63 m) for boys and 5 feet 3 inches (1.60 m) for girls. The average weight is 107 pounds (48.6 kg) for boys and 108 pounds (49.1 kg) for girls. Boys have now caught up with girls in terms of height, but not weight.

GROWN-UP

By the age of 18 girls are generally fully grown, whereas boys will keep on growing for another couple of years. Boys are taller and heavier than girls. Boys' average height is 5 feet 9 inches (1.75 m) and their average weight is 143 pounds (65 kg). The girls' average height is 5 feet 4 inches (1.63 m) and their average weight is 120 pounds (54.6 kg). Individuals are developing an adult sense of identity, and forming more mature relationships with people of their own age and with their parents.

Glossary

A

ABDOMEN The part of the body between the diaphragm and the hips. The abdomen contains the stomach, intestines, kidneys, and bladder.

ABSORPTION Taking digested food into the bloodstream through the wall of the small intestine.

ADRENAL GLAND One of two glands that produce many hormones, including adrenaline, and are found on top of each kidney.

ANTIBODY A chemical produced by lymphocytes that helps destroy invading disease-causing organisms.

ANUS The lower end of the digestive system, through which undigested food is pushed out.

AORTA The body's largest artery, which carries blood from the heart to the body.

ARTERY A blood vessel that carries blood away from the heart.

ATRIUM One of two atria, the upper chambers of the heart.

B

BACTERIA A group of very simple, one-celled organisms. Some types cause diseases such as pneumonia and typhoid in humans.

BILE A liquid produced in the liver, stored in the gall bladder, and released into the small intestine to help digest fats.

BLADDER A muscular, elastic bag that stores urine produced by the kidneys until it is ready for release.

BLOOD A liquid tissue that circulates around the body in tubes called blood vessels. It consists of a liquid part, plasma, in which red and white blood cells are suspended.

BONE A piece of supporting tissue that consists of collagen fibres, to give it elasticity, and mineral salts, such as calcium, to give it hardness.

C

CANINE A type of tooth used for gripping and tearing food.

CAPILLARY The smallest type of blood vessel. Millions of capillaries carry blood to, and from, all the body's cells.

CARBON DIOXIDE A kind of gas found in the air. We breathe out more carbon dioxide than we breathe in because it is released during respiration inside all cells.

CARTILAGE A flexible structural tissue found, for example, covering the ends of bones in joints, and supporting the ear and nose.

CELL One of the millions of basic building blocks that makes up the human body, and the bodies of all other organisms.

CENTRAL NERVOUS SYSTEM (CNS) The brain and the spinal cord.

CEREBELLUM The part of the brain that produces smooth, coordinated movements.

CEREBRUM The largest part of the brain. It is responsible for thought, language, learning, memory and personality.

COCHLEA A snail-shaped, coiled tube in the inner part of the ear that contains sound receptors.

CONES Cells found in the retina of the eye that are sensitive to colored light.

CONNECTIVE TISSUE A type of tissue that supports organs and forms tendons and ligaments.

D

DEOXYRIBONUCLEIC ACID (DNA) The substance found in all cells that carries a person's genetic information.

DERMIS The inner part of the skin, below the epidermis. It contains blood capillaries and nerve endings.

D

DIAPHRAGM The muscle sheet that separates the chest (or thorax) from the abdomen. The diaphragm plays an important role in breathing.

DIGESTION The process of breaking down large food molecules into smaller food molecules that can then be absorbed into the bloodstream by the body.

E

ELECTROCARDIOGRAM (ECG) A record, in the form of a graph, of the electrical activity of the heart.

EMBRYO The name given to a developing baby up to the end of its eighth week inside the uterus.

ENDOCRINE GLAND A gland that produces hormones.

ENZYME A substance that speeds up chemical reactions. Digestive enzymes speed up the breakdown of food during digestion.

EPIDERMIS The outer part of the skin, above the dermis.

EPIGLOTTIS A flap at the back of the throat that covers the entrance to the windpipe during swallowing.

ESOPHAGUS The part of the digestive system that carries food from the mouth to the stomach.

F

FETUS The name given to a developing baby between its eighth week in the uterus and its birth.

FERTILIZATION The joining of a sperm and egg.

G

GALL BLADDER A small bag behind the liver in which bile is stored prior to release into the small intestine.

GLAND An organ specialized to produce a substance either for further use inside the body (e.g. a salivary gland producing saliva) or for elimination (e.g. a sweat gland producing sweat).

H

HEART The four-chambered muscular pump that pushes blood around the body.

HEMOGLOBIN An orange substance found inside red blood cells that carries oxygen.

HORMONE A chemical "messenger" released into the blood by an endocrine gland to cause a change elsewhere in the body.

I

INCISOR A type of tooth used for biting off chunks of food.

INTESTINE The long tubular section of the digestive system that fills most of the abdomen. In the small intestine, the first and longer section, food is digested and absorbed. The shorter large intestine carries waste to the outside.

IRIS The colored part of the eye that surrounds, and controls the size of, the pupil.

J

JOINT The place where two or more bones meet.

K

KIDNEY One of two organs found in the upper abdomen that remove waste from the blood and produce urine.

L

LARYNX The organ that lies between the throat and windpipe and produces sounds.

LIGAMENT The tough tissue that holds bones together at joints.

LIVER A large organ, found in the abdomen, in which hundreds of chemical processes take place, many linked to digestion.

LUMEN The cavity inside a blood vessel or other type of tube inside the body.

LUNGS The spongy organs found inside the chest in which oxygen is exchanged for carbon dioxide.

LYMPH Excess fluid draining into the tissues from blood capillaries and carried away by the lymph system.

LYMPH NODE One of many small organs in the lymph system that filters disease-causing organisms out of the lymph.

LYMPHOCYTE A type of white blood cell that produces antibodies.

M

MENSTRUATION The breakdown and loss of the lining of the uterus each month that occurs if an egg has not been fertilized.

MOLAR A type of tooth used for crushing and chewing food.

MONOCYTE A type of white blood cell that eats bacteria and other foreign bodies.

MUCUS A slimy secretion produced by various parts of the body including nose and mouth.

MUSCLE A type of tissue that can contract, or get shorter.

N

NEPHRON One of millions of filtration units that remove waste from blood flowing through the kidneys.

NERVE A long cylindrical tissue that carries nerve impulses to and from the central nervous system.

NEURON A nerve cell. A nerve is made up of many neurons.

NEUTROPHIL A type of white blood cell that eats bacteria and other foreign bodies.

O

ORGAN A collection of tissues that work together to carry out a particular function; for example, the kidney.

ORGANELLE A microscopic structure inside a cell that carries out a particular function.

OSSICLES The three tiny bones in the middle ear that carry sounds from the outer ear to the cochlea.

OVARY A female sex organ in which eggs and sex hormones are produced.

OXYGEN A kind of gas. Oxygen is breathed in and used by body cells to release energy from food molecules during respiration.

P

PALATE The roof of the mouth.

PANCREAS A gland found below the stomach that produces hormones, and enzymes involved in digestion.

PHARYNX The muscular tube that links the nose and mouth to the windpipe and esophagus.

PITUITARY GLAND A tiny pea-sized gland found below the brain that produces hormones that control many other hormone-producing glands inside the body.

PLACENTA The organ that links a developing fetus to its mother.

PLASMA The liquid part of blood in which blood cells are suspended.

PLATELET A cell fragment found in blood that plays an important part in clotting.

PREMOLAR A type of tooth used for crushing and chewing food.

PULSE The rhythmic expansion of an artery that happens with each heartbeat. A pulse can be felt where the artery passes over a bone.

PUPIL The black hole in the front of the eye through which light enters.

R

RESPIRATION The process occurring inside all body cells by which oxygen is used to release energy from fuel molecules such as glucose. Carbon dioxide is released as waste, and is breathed out.

RETINA The light-sensitive layer that covers the inside of the eye. Nerve fibers from the retina carry impulses to the brain.

RODS Cells found in the retina of the eye that are sensitive to dim light.

S

SALIVA A liquid involved in digestion that is produced by salivary glands surrounding the mouth.

SEMICIRCULAR CANALS A part of the inner ear that enables us to balance.

SKELETON The bones of the body that together support it. Some bones also protect delicate organs such as the brain, lungs, and heart.

SPERM A male reproductive cell, produced in the testes. A sperm fuses with the female egg during fertilization.

SPHINCTER A ring of muscle that controls flow of liquid through a system. An example is the pyloric sphincter that controls the flow of food from the stomach into the small intestine.

SPINAL CORD The part of the central nervous system that links the brain with the rest of the body.

STOMACH A part of the digestive system in the form of a muscular bag that lies between the esophagus and the small intestine.

SYSTEM A collection of organs that work together to carry out a particular function; for example, the digestive system.

T

TASTE BUD One of many thousands of tiny structures in the tongue that detects flavors.

TENDON A tough, inelastic band of fibers that links a muscle to a bone.

TESTIS One of two male sex organs in which sperm and sex hormones are produced.

THORAX The part of the body between neck and diaphragm. The thorax contains the lungs and heart.

TISSUE A collection of similar cells that performs a particular function; for example, muscle tissue.

TRACHEA The tube, surrounded and strengthened by rings of cartilage, that carries air from the throat to the lungs.

U

UREA A waste substance produced in the liver, and excreted from the body, in the urine, by the kidneys.

URINE A waste fluid produced by the kidneys. It consists mainly of water, but also contains dissolved wastes including urea.

UTERUS A hollow, thick-walled organ that is part of the female reproductive system in which an embryo develops.

V

VALVE A structure found inside veins and the heart. A valve stops blood flowing backward and ensures that it flows around the body in one direction only.

VEIN A type of blood vessel that carries blood toward the heart.

VENA CAVA The body's largest vein, which carries blood from the body to the heart.

VENTRICLE One of the two lower chambers of the heart.

VOCAL CORDS Two folds of tissue in the larynx that are moved and stretched to produce sounds.

Index

Acknowledgments

Quarto would like to thank the following for providing photographs, and for granting permission to reproduce copyright material:

Barts Medical Illustration: 25br; Roger Chester:Bubbles: 27al; Mike Evans:Life File: 50bl; Eye Ubiquitous:TRIP: 47br; Jacqui Farrow:Bubbles: 17cl, 17bl, 17bc, 27bcr, 31ar, 56ar; Carol Fulton:Bubbles: 55br; Andrew Gasson: 42ar; Brian Gibbs:TRIP: 45ar; Institute of Laryngology & Otology Photographic Department: 26cl, 46br; Martin Jackson:Bubbles: 36br; Brian Lake:TRIP: 13bl, 41ca; National Medical Slide Bank: 18c, 19bl, 22br, 23al, 52ar, 53ar; NASA:TRIP: 36ac; Oxford Scientific Films: 13al, 13ar, 13br, 18cr, 18bc, 18br, 31br, 36ar, 37cl, 38cl, 40ar, 40cl, 41al, 41bl, 47bl; Claire Paxton:Bubbles: 27bl; Quarto: 6, 7; H.C.Robinson:Bubbles: 49ar; Helene Rogers:TRIP: 10ar, 10cl, 10bl, 10br, 18cl, 23bc, 27ar, 27bcl, 29al, 29ar, 29bl, 29br, 35al, 41ra, 41rc, 41rb, 41c, 49br, 55ar; Frans Rombout:Bubbles: 23cr, 53br; David Simson:das PHOTO: 25ar; J.M.Steinlein:Bubbles: 36bc; Loisjoy Thurston:Bubbles: 21bl, 30ar, 31cr, 36cr; TRIP: 10cr, 15ar, 36cl; Flora Torrance:TRIP: 24bc, 44bl; Bob Turner:TRIP: 10al; Ian West:Bubbles: 19al, 27br, 28ar, 28bl, 41cb; Jennie Woodcock:Bubbles: 17al, 36bl.

(a = above, b = below, c = center, l = left, r = right)

While every effort has been made to trace and acknowledge all copyright holders, we would like to apologize should any omissions have been made.